Ivy Global

# New SAT Practice Test 1

 + 💬

Resources & Downloads:

IVYGLOBAL.COM/STUDY

PASSWORD: greenbook

# NEW SAT PRACTICE TEST 1

This publication was written and edited by the team at Ivy Global.

Editors-in-Chief: Corwin Henville and Kristin Rose
Producers: Lloyd Min and Junho Suh

Editors: Sacha Azor, Nathan Létourneau, and Sarah Pike

Contributors: Alexandra Candib, Cathleen Childs, Natalia Cole, Laurel Durning-Hammond, Lei Huang, Caroline Incledon, Somin Lee, and Mark Mendola

This product was developed by Ivy Global, a pioneering education company that delivers a wide range of educational services.

E-mail: publishing@ivyglobal.com
Website: http://www.ivyglobal.com

# Part 1
# Introduction

# HOW TO USE THIS BOOKLET

Welcome, students and parents! This booklet is intended to help students prepare for the SAT, a test administered by the College Board. It contains an overview of the SAT, a few basic test-taking tips, a full-length practice test, and an answer key and scoring directions.

The first key to succeeding on the SAT is to know the test. This booklet will help you know what to expect and build your confidence. Reading the quick tips in this booklet can help you to avoid common mistakes. Taking this practice test will help you to become more familiar with the format, pacing, and content of the exam. Reviewing your scores, as well as any questions you missed, can help you determine what you might need to continue studying in order to do your best on test day.

This booklet is not a totally comprehensive test-prep book: for a comprehensive study guide to the SAT, we recommend Ivy Global's New SAT Guide.

## THE TEST

The SAT is a test used by most US colleges to help make admissions decisions. It is administered in 5 sections: the Reading section, the Math (No Calculator) section, the Writing and Language section, the Math (Calculator) section, and the optional Essay. Most questions on the SAT are multiple choice, with four answer options. Some problems in the Math section are student-produced response questions; rather than selecting from a list of answer options, you will have to solve a problem and enter a number on your answer sheet. The Essay is a writing assignment, and you will be given lined paper to write your essay.

The SAT is a timed exam. You will be allowed a limited amount of time for each section. Set aside a total of 4 hours for this exam. The amount of time that you will have for each section is given on the first page of each section. If you are taking a proctored exam, your proctor will also announce the time that you are allowed for each section.

Detailed directions are provided at the beginning of each section. Read these directions carefully when taking practice exams. You should try to be totally familiar with the directions for each section by the time that you take the real SAT.

# QUICK TIPS

Read every question and all answer options carefully. Many students select incorrect answers when they could easily find the correct answers simply because they misread the questions or don't look at all of the answer options. Read carefully to avoid careless errors.

Use the process of elimination. Sometimes the easiest way to find the correct answer is to cross out the answers in your test booklet that you can be sure are incorrect. Don't cross answers out on your answer sheet, as stray marks could be counted as incorrect answers.

Make your best guess on every problem. You should always try to find the correct answer, but if you find that you're stumped then you should try to make your best guess. There's no penalty for guessing.

Don't be afraid to write in your test booklet, but always remember to mark you answer on your answer sheet. The scorers won't look at your test booklet: you won't get points off for writing in it, or receive credit for showing your work.

Download printable answer sheets, answer keys, and Excel scoring sheets from:
ivyglobal.com/study

Part 2
# Practice Test

# SAT Practice Test – General Directions

This exam is a diagnostic to help you assess your strengths and weaknesses for the new SAT.

## Format

- The SAT is 3 hours long, or 3 hours and 50 minutes with the optional Essay.
- The test is composed of the following sections:
    - o 65-minute Reading section
    - o 25-minute Math section (No-calculator)
    - o 35-minute Writing and Language section
    - o 55-minute Math section (Calculator)
    - o 50-minute Optional Essay-writing section

## Answering Questions

- Mark your answers in your answer sheet.
- Make sure to fill in each bubble completely.
- Use a No. 2 pencil.
- Make sure you are filling in the correct section of the answer sheet.
- Do not make stray marks on your answer sheet.
- For the optional Essay use the lined paper provided.

## Using Your Test Booklet

- You are not given credit for any answers or work shown in the test booklet. Feel free to use your booklet for scratchwork.
- You may not transfer answers from the test booklet to your answer sheet after time has elapsed on a section.
- You may not fold or remove pages, or take home any part of the test.

## DO NOT BEGIN THE PRACTICE TEST
## UNTIL YOUR PROCTOR TELLS YOU TO DO SO.

Download printable answer sheets, answer keys, and Excel scoring sheets from:

ivyglobal.com/study

**Your Name (Print):** _____

Last                   First

**SECTION 1**

| | | | | | |
|---|---|---|---|---|---|
| 1 Ⓐ Ⓑ Ⓒ Ⓓ | 11 Ⓐ Ⓑ Ⓒ Ⓓ | 21 Ⓐ Ⓑ Ⓒ Ⓓ | 31 Ⓐ Ⓑ Ⓒ Ⓓ | 41 Ⓐ Ⓑ Ⓒ Ⓓ | 51 Ⓐ Ⓑ Ⓒ Ⓓ |
| 2 Ⓐ Ⓑ Ⓒ Ⓓ | 12 Ⓐ Ⓑ Ⓒ Ⓓ | 22 Ⓐ Ⓑ Ⓒ Ⓓ | 32 Ⓐ Ⓑ Ⓒ Ⓓ | 42 Ⓐ Ⓑ Ⓒ Ⓓ | 52 Ⓐ Ⓑ Ⓒ Ⓓ |
| 3 Ⓐ Ⓑ Ⓒ Ⓓ | 13 Ⓐ Ⓑ Ⓒ Ⓓ | 23 Ⓐ Ⓑ Ⓒ Ⓓ | 33 Ⓐ Ⓑ Ⓒ Ⓓ | 43 Ⓐ Ⓑ Ⓒ Ⓓ | |
| 4 Ⓐ Ⓑ Ⓒ Ⓓ | 14 Ⓐ Ⓑ Ⓒ Ⓓ | 24 Ⓐ Ⓑ Ⓒ Ⓓ | 34 Ⓐ Ⓑ Ⓒ Ⓓ | 44 Ⓐ Ⓑ Ⓒ Ⓓ | |
| 5 Ⓐ Ⓑ Ⓒ Ⓓ | 15 Ⓐ Ⓑ Ⓒ Ⓓ | 25 Ⓐ Ⓑ Ⓒ Ⓓ | 35 Ⓐ Ⓑ Ⓒ Ⓓ | 45 Ⓐ Ⓑ Ⓒ Ⓓ | |
| 6 Ⓐ Ⓑ Ⓒ Ⓓ | 16 Ⓐ Ⓑ Ⓒ Ⓓ | 26 Ⓐ Ⓑ Ⓒ Ⓓ | 36 Ⓐ Ⓑ Ⓒ Ⓓ | 46 Ⓐ Ⓑ Ⓒ Ⓓ | |
| 7 Ⓐ Ⓑ Ⓒ Ⓓ | 17 Ⓐ Ⓑ Ⓒ Ⓓ | 27 Ⓐ Ⓑ Ⓒ Ⓓ | 37 Ⓐ Ⓑ Ⓒ Ⓓ | 47 Ⓐ Ⓑ Ⓒ Ⓓ | |
| 8 Ⓐ Ⓑ Ⓒ Ⓓ | 18 Ⓐ Ⓑ Ⓒ Ⓓ | 28 Ⓐ Ⓑ Ⓒ Ⓓ | 38 Ⓐ Ⓑ Ⓒ Ⓓ | 48 Ⓐ Ⓑ Ⓒ Ⓓ | |
| 9 Ⓐ Ⓑ Ⓒ Ⓓ | 19 Ⓐ Ⓑ Ⓒ Ⓓ | 29 Ⓐ Ⓑ Ⓒ Ⓓ | 39 Ⓐ Ⓑ Ⓒ Ⓓ | 49 Ⓐ Ⓑ Ⓒ Ⓓ | |
| 10 Ⓐ Ⓑ Ⓒ Ⓓ | 20 Ⓐ Ⓑ Ⓒ Ⓓ | 30 Ⓐ Ⓑ Ⓒ Ⓓ | 40 Ⓐ Ⓑ Ⓒ Ⓓ | 50 Ⓐ Ⓑ Ⓒ Ⓓ | |

**SECTION 2**

| | |
|---|---|
| 1 Ⓐ Ⓑ Ⓒ Ⓓ | 11 Ⓐ Ⓑ Ⓒ Ⓓ |
| 2 Ⓐ Ⓑ Ⓒ Ⓓ | 12 Ⓐ Ⓑ Ⓒ Ⓓ |
| 3 Ⓐ Ⓑ Ⓒ Ⓓ | 13 Ⓐ Ⓑ Ⓒ Ⓓ |
| 4 Ⓐ Ⓑ Ⓒ Ⓓ | 14 Ⓐ Ⓑ Ⓒ Ⓓ |
| 5 Ⓐ Ⓑ Ⓒ Ⓓ | 15 Ⓐ Ⓑ Ⓒ Ⓓ |
| 6 Ⓐ Ⓑ Ⓒ Ⓓ | |
| 7 Ⓐ Ⓑ Ⓒ Ⓓ | |
| 8 Ⓐ Ⓑ Ⓒ Ⓓ | |
| 9 Ⓐ Ⓑ Ⓒ Ⓓ | |
| 10 Ⓐ Ⓑ Ⓒ Ⓓ | |

16    17    18    19    20

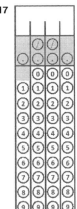
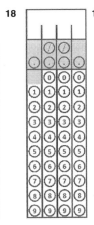
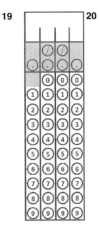
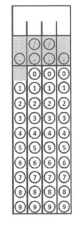

**SECTION 3**

| | | | | |
|---|---|---|---|---|
| 1 Ⓐ Ⓑ Ⓒ Ⓓ | 11 Ⓐ Ⓑ Ⓒ Ⓓ | 21 Ⓐ Ⓑ Ⓒ Ⓓ | 31 Ⓐ Ⓑ Ⓒ Ⓓ | 41 Ⓐ Ⓑ Ⓒ Ⓓ |
| 2 Ⓐ Ⓑ Ⓒ Ⓓ | 12 Ⓐ Ⓑ Ⓒ Ⓓ | 22 Ⓐ Ⓑ Ⓒ Ⓓ | 32 Ⓐ Ⓑ Ⓒ Ⓓ | 42 Ⓐ Ⓑ Ⓒ Ⓓ |
| 3 Ⓐ Ⓑ Ⓒ Ⓓ | 13 Ⓐ Ⓑ Ⓒ Ⓓ | 23 Ⓐ Ⓑ Ⓒ Ⓓ | 33 Ⓐ Ⓑ Ⓒ Ⓓ | 43 Ⓐ Ⓑ Ⓒ Ⓓ |
| 4 Ⓐ Ⓑ Ⓒ Ⓓ | 14 Ⓐ Ⓑ Ⓒ Ⓓ | 24 Ⓐ Ⓑ Ⓒ Ⓓ | 34 Ⓐ Ⓑ Ⓒ Ⓓ | 44 Ⓐ Ⓑ Ⓒ Ⓓ |
| 5 Ⓐ Ⓑ Ⓒ Ⓓ | 15 Ⓐ Ⓑ Ⓒ Ⓓ | 25 Ⓐ Ⓑ Ⓒ Ⓓ | 35 Ⓐ Ⓑ Ⓒ Ⓓ | |
| 6 Ⓐ Ⓑ Ⓒ Ⓓ | 16 Ⓐ Ⓑ Ⓒ Ⓓ | 26 Ⓐ Ⓑ Ⓒ Ⓓ | 36 Ⓐ Ⓑ Ⓒ Ⓓ | |
| 7 Ⓐ Ⓑ Ⓒ Ⓓ | 17 Ⓐ Ⓑ Ⓒ Ⓓ | 27 Ⓐ Ⓑ Ⓒ Ⓓ | 37 Ⓐ Ⓑ Ⓒ Ⓓ | |
| 8 Ⓐ Ⓑ Ⓒ Ⓓ | 18 Ⓐ Ⓑ Ⓒ Ⓓ | 28 Ⓐ Ⓑ Ⓒ Ⓓ | 38 Ⓐ Ⓑ Ⓒ Ⓓ | |
| 9 Ⓐ Ⓑ Ⓒ Ⓓ | 19 Ⓐ Ⓑ Ⓒ Ⓓ | 29 Ⓐ Ⓑ Ⓒ Ⓓ | 39 Ⓐ Ⓑ Ⓒ Ⓓ | |
| 10 Ⓐ Ⓑ Ⓒ Ⓓ | 20 Ⓐ Ⓑ Ⓒ Ⓓ | 30 Ⓐ Ⓑ Ⓒ Ⓓ | 40 Ⓐ Ⓑ Ⓒ Ⓓ | |

## SECTION

# 4

1 (A) (B) (C) (D)
2 (A) (B) (C) (D)
3 (A) (B) (C) (D)
4 (A) (B) (C) (D)
5 (A) (B) (C) (D)
6 (A) (B) (C) (D)
7 (A) (B) (C) (D)
8 (A) (B) (C) (D)
9 (A) (B) (C) (D)
10 (A) (B) (C) (D)

11 (A) (B) (C) (D)
12 (A) (B) (C) (D)
13 (A) (B) (C) (D)
14 (A) (B) (C) (D)
15 (A) (B) (C) (D)
16 (A) (B) (C) (D)
17 (A) (B) (C) (D)
18 (A) (B) (C) (D)
19 (A) (B) (C) (D)
20 (A) (B) (C) (D)

21 (A) (B) (C) (D)
22 (A) (B) (C) (D)
23 (A) (B) (C) (D)
24 (A) (B) (C) (D)
25 (A) (B) (C) (D)
26 (A) (B) (C) (D)
27 (A) (B) (C) (D)
28 (A) (B) (C) (D)
29 (A) (B) (C) (D)
30 (A) (B) (C) (D)

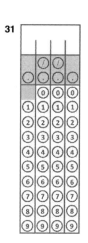

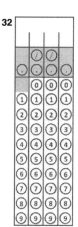

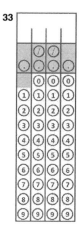

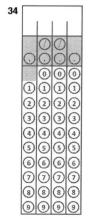

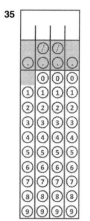

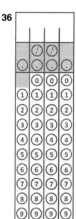

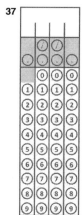

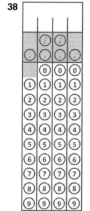

**IMPORTANT**: USE A NO. 2 PENCIL. WRITE INSIDE THE BORDERS.

**Continue on next page.**

**Continue on next page.**

**Continue on next page.**

**Continue on next page.**

# Section 1

# SECTION 1

**Time – 65 minutes**
**52 Questions**

---

**Turn to Section 1 of your answer sheet to answer the questions in this section.**

---

**Directions:** For these questions, determine the solution to each question presented and choose the best answer choice of those provided. Be sure to fill in the respective circle on your answer sheet.

---

**Questions 1-11 are based on the following passage.**

*This passage is adapted from Atul Grover, "Should Hospital Residency Programs Be Expanded to Increase the Number of Doctors?" © 2013 Dow Jones & Company.*

Thanks to baby boomers, the population over 65 will have doubled between 2000 and 2030. And when the Affordable Care Act takes full effect, up to 32 million new patients will seek access to medical care, many of whom will
5 need treatment for ailments that have gone undiagnosed for years, such as cancer, diabetes, arthritis and heart disease. This surge in demand means the U.S. will have a shortfall of at least 90,000 doctors by the end of the decade, according to the Association of American Medical Colleges Center for
10 Workforce Studies. Many parts of the country have too few doctors already.

A small, vocal minority of researchers suggest we don't need more doctors. That minority clearly is having an impact: many clinicians and policy makers say there is 20%
15 to 30% "waste" in our health-care system. Elliott Fisher, a Dartmouth professor, says those numbers are backed up by Dartmouth research.

The Dartmouth studies base their conclusions about waste on comparisons of health-care spending in different
20 geographic areas. But other studies have shown that differences in the health status of patients in the different regions explain the majority of variations in spending. In other words, urban areas, with their high concentrations of poor people, tend to have a higher disease burden and thus
25 higher medical needs. Sicker patients, along with high labor costs, explain the higher levels of spending found in these urban areas—not too many doctors.

There is no question that delivery of care needs to be better organized, and that some current reforms are likely to

30 improve patient outcomes. That's true, for example, with experiments in team-based care. However, these improvements in patient care have not translated to any reduction in the need for physician time.

Another new experiment–accountable-care organizations,
35 which allow groups of providers to share any savings gained by keeping their patients healthy–also hasn't been shown to reduce the number of physicians needed. Indeed, there is a lot of wishful thinking associated with ACOs, just as there was with HMOs[1] in the 1990s—that everyone would be
40 cared for in a way that would cost less and would prevent people from ever getting sick. Unfortunately, that didn't turn out to be the reality.

Primary care and prevention will increase the need for doctors. An 8-year-old girl with acute leukemia today has an
45 80% chance of survival. If she survives, in the years that follow, she is likely to get a vaccine to avoid cervical cancer, take cholesterol-lowering drugs and undergo multiple screenings for breast cancer. She may still develop heart disease or cancer. And as she and millions of other people
50 continue to age, their risk for other conditions like Alzheimer's will increase dramatically. But she, like everyone else, deserves first-rate care every step of the way. We need more doctors, not fewer.

---

[1] Health maintenance organizations

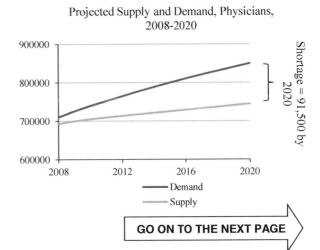

Projected Supply and Demand, Physicians, 2008-2020

**GO ON TO THE NEXT PAGE**

1. Which of the following provides the best summary of the passage's main idea?

   (A) The US health care system is about to suffer a significant collapse, and hundreds of hospitals will have to be shut down.
   (B) There is too much wasteful spending in the current health care system, which additional doctors cannot correct.
   (C) The US needs to prepare for increasing health care demands by training more doctors.
   (D) Accountable care organizations (ACOs) will improve the current health care system and reduce unnecessary care.

2. The author argues that the US will experience a shortfall of doctors because

   (A) a large portion of doctors are choosing to retire early.
   (B) new legislation and an aging population will increase the demand for healthcare.
   (C) many doctors waste too much of their time on non-essential treatments rather than more important ailments.
   (D) many medical programs have closed and fewer doctors are being trained.

3. Which choice provides the best evidence for the answer to the previous question?

   (A) Lines 7-10 ("This surge … Studies")
   (B) Lines 13-15 ("That minority … system")
   (C) Lines 22-25 ("In other … needs")
   (D) Lines 45-48 ("If she … cancer")

4. The passage most strongly suggests that

   (A) primary care and prevention, while important, will not solve the issue of a doctor shortage.
   (B) preventing diseases via primary care will help reduce costs for healthcare by reducing early death.
   (C) relocating doctors from urban to rural areas will reduce US medical costs.
   (D) the first step in resolving the doctor shortage is conducting more extensive research on its causes.

5. Which choice provides the best evidence for the answer to the previous question?

   (A) Lines 20-22 ("But other … spending")
   (B) Lines 25-27 ("Sicker patients … doctors")
   (C) Lines 31-33 ("However these … time")
   (D) Lines 43-44 ("Primary care … doctors")

6. As used in line 12, "vocal" most nearly means

   (A) blunt.
   (B) outspoken.
   (C) out loud.
   (D) forthright.

7. The passage suggests that the 20%-30% "waste" mentioned in lines 14-17 is

   (A) likely to result in a reduction in the demand for physician time.
   (B) a significant expense, but still less expensive than the cost of training enough new doctors.
   (C) mostly explained by differences in patient health, rather than wasteful spending.
   (D) best explained by the fact that affluent patients tend to spend more on healthcare.

8. The primary purpose of the fifth paragraph (lines 34-42) is to

   (A) discuss another potential option to mitigate the coming shortage in physicians.
   (B) offer a historical account of physicians' various organizations.
   (C) provide evidence that the government is coming up with clever options to address problems in healthcare.
   (D) support the author's claim that new experiments in patient care will not solve the coming doctor shortage.

9. As used in line 44, "acute" most nearly means

   (A) critical.
   (B) keen.
   (C) severe.
   (D) sharp.

**GO ON TO THE NEXT PAGE** ⟩

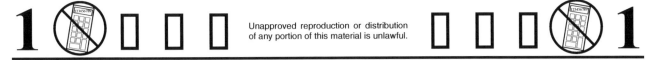

10. Which of the following best expresses the main point of the final paragraph (lines 43-53)?

(A) Even though patients may live longer, primary and preventative care still offer savings.

(B) We must provide the highest quality of care possible, in order to reduce costs.

(C) The shortage of physicians is best explained by an excessive amount of primary care.

(D) Although we have a responsibility to provide high-quality care, we should not expect for that to decrease medical costs.

11. Which of the following claims is best supported by the graph?

(A) There will be more doctors in 2020 than at any time since 2008, and a greater shortage of doctors.

(B) The doctor shortage will continue to grow until there are 91,500 fewer doctors in 2020 than there were in 2008.

(C) By 2015, around 850,000 patients will need a doctor, but only about 750,000 will receive any form of treatment.

(D) An increase in the supply of doctors over time will cause an even greater increase in the demand.

GO ON TO THE NEXT PAGE

**Questions 12-22 are based on the following passages.**

*The following passages are adapted from Chensheng Lu and Janet H. Silverstein, "Would Americans Be Better Off Eating an Organic Diet?" © 2014 by Dow Jones & Company.*

**Passage 1**

Is there definitive scientific proof that an organic diet is healthier? Not yet. Robust scientific studies comparing food grown organically and food grown conventionally don't exist, thanks to a lack of funding for this kind of research in
5    humans.

But let's be clear: Some convincing scientific work does exist to suggest that an organic diet has its benefits. What's more, it only makes sense that food free of pesticides and chemicals is safer and better for us than food
10   containing those substances, even at trace levels. This was illustrated in a study published in the journal Environmental Health Perspectives in 2006. That study, which I led, showed that within five days of substituting mostly organic produce in children's diets for conventional produce, pesticides
15   disappeared from the children's urine.

Many say the pesticides found in our food are nothing to fear because the levels fall well below federal safety guidelines and thus aren't dangerous. Similarly, they say the bovine growth hormone used to increase cows' milk yield is
20   perfectly safe. But federal guidelines don't take into account what effect repeated exposure to low levels of chemicals might have on humans over time. And many pesticides were eventually banned or restricted by the federal government after years of use when they were discovered to be harmful
25   to the environment or human health.

Organic skeptics like to cite a meta-analysis study published in the Annals of Internal Medicine last year that suggested organic foods are neither healthier nor more nutritious than their conventional counterparts. Left out of
30   that analysis, however, were recent field studies showing that organic produce, such as strawberries, leafy vegetables, and wheat, not only tastes better but contains much higher levels of phenolic acids than conventional produce. Phenolic acids are secondary plant metabolites that can be absorbed easily
35   through the walls of the intestinal tract, and can act as potent antioxidants that prevent cellular damage, and therefore offer some protection against oxidative stress, inflammation, and cancer. Knowing that we could reduce our exposure to pesticides and increase our exposure to antioxidants by
40   eating organic food, it makes great common sense to consume more of it.

**Passage 2**

There is no definitive evidence that organic food is more nutritious or healthier than conventional food, but there is proof that eating more fruits and vegetables and less
45   processed food is.

Therefore, our focus as a society should be to eat as much fresh food and whole grains as possible—regardless of whether it is organically grown or not.

It is difficult to compare the nutritional value of organic
50   versus conventional food because the soil, climate, timing of harvest, and storage conditions all affect the composition of produce. Still, published studies have found no significant differences in nutritional quality between organic and nonorganic produce or milk. Similarly, there is no evidence
55   that giving bovine growth hormone (BGH) to cows changes the composition of milk or affects human health. BGH is inactive in humans and degrades in the acidic environment of the stomach.

As for pesticide exposure, the U.S. in 1996 established
60   maximum permissible levels for pesticide residues in food to ensure food safety. Many studies have shown that pesticide levels in conventional produce fall well below those guidelines. While it's true that organic fruits and vegetables in general contain fewer traces of these chemicals, we can't
65   draw conclusions about what that means for health as there haven't been any long-term studies comparing the relationship between exposure to pesticides from organic versus nonorganic foods and adverse health outcomes. It may seem like "common sense" to reduce exposure to these
70   chemicals, but there are currently no good evidence-based studies to answer the question.

We would like to think that organic food is grown locally, put in a wheelbarrow and brought directly to our homes. However, much of it comes from countries where
75   regulations might not be as tightly enforced as in the U.S., and labeling of the foods might be misleading. And just because food is labeled organic doesn't mean it is completely free of pesticides. Contamination can occur from soil and ground water containing previously used chemicals, or
80   during transport, processing and storage. Organochlorine insecticides were recently found in organically grown root crops and tomatoes even though these pesticides haven't been used for 20 years.

Given what we know, the best diet advice we can give
85   families is to eat a wide variety of produce and whole grains. Whether they want to buy organic is up to them.

**GO ON TO THE NEXT PAGE**

12. The author's main purpose in Passage 1 appears to be to

(A) discuss the implications of new research into the health effects of organic foods.
(B) persuade readers that eating organic food has potential health benefits.
(C) critique research which claims to show that there are no health benefits from eating organic food.
(D) argue that more funding is required to perform better research about organic food.

13. The first passage most strongly suggests that

(A) study results conflict on some points, but agree that it is healthiest to eat an all-organic diet.
(B) organic diets have unique health benefits, despite some incomplete studies that claim the contrary.
(C) all studies conducted on humans show that organic diets are essential to health.
(D) studies are inconclusive regarding the benefits of an organic diet, except when it comes to the diets of children.

14. Which choice within Passage 1 provides the best evidence for the answer to the previous question?

(A) Lines 2-5 ("Robust scientific ... humans")
(B) Lines 12-15 ("That study ... urine")
(C) Lines 22-25 ("And many ... health")
(D) Lines 29-33 ("Left out ... produce")

15. The attitude of the author of Passage 2 towards health claims about organic foods would best be described as

(A) derisive.
(B) skeptical.
(C) enthusiastic.
(D) quizzical.

16. As used in line 42 within Passage 2, "definitive" most nearly means

(A) conclusive.
(B) consummate.
(C) accepted.
(D) specific.

17. As used in line 68, "adverse" most nearly means

(A) harmful.
(B) antagonistic.
(C) unlucky.
(D) contrary.

18. The author's purpose in lines 72-74 within Passage 2 ("We would ... homes") is most likely to

(A) provide a detailed description of the process that most people believe is implied by organic labeling.
(B) characterize the organic food industry as inefficient and unsophisticated.
(C) caricature misconceptions about organic food to help create a stark contrast with reality.
(D) offer a vision for how organic agriculture could operate if the author's recommendations are adopted.

19. Passage 1 differs from Passage 2 in that

(A) Passage 1 argues that only organic foods should be eaten, while Passage 2 argues that only non-organic foods should be.
(B) Passage 1 argues that people should consume more organic foods, while Passage 2 states that it is more important to focus on eating a less processed diet.
(C) Passage 1 argues that organic foods are important for health, while Passage 2 argues they are harmful.
(D) Passage 1 argues that organic foods are overemphasized in the media, while Passage 2 argues they are not emphasized enough.

20. The authors of both passages would most likely agree with which of the following statements?

(A) It is reasonable to conclude that long-term exposure to even low levels of pesticides has a negative effect on human health.
(B) Scientific studies on organic foods cannot be trusted, as they often conflict with one another.
(C) Food labels are highly variable and all but useless, and it is better to select foods based on their freshness.
(D) There is enough information available about the health impacts of various foods to enable informed decisions about diet.

**GO ON TO THE NEXT PAGE**

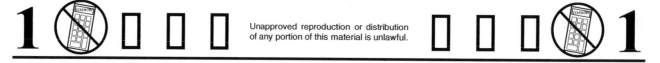
1

Unapproved reproduction or distribution
of any portion of this material is unlawful.

1

21. Based on the two passages, which best describes the relationship between organic food and health risks?

(A) Organic foods offer nutritional benefits which more than offset their health risks.

(B) Organic foods clearly protect against a variety of known health risks.

(C) Organic foods have a reputation for being healthy, but actually increase certain risks.

(D) Organic foods may reduce exposure to possible but unconfirmed health risks.

22. Which choice provides the best evidence for the answer to the previous question?

(A) Lines 46-48 ("Therefore, our ... not")

(B) Lines 63-68 ("While it's ... outcomes")

(C) Lines 72-74 ("We would ... homes")

(D) Lines 80-83 ("Organochlorine insecticides ... years")

**GO ON TO THE NEXT PAGE**

Practice Test 1

**Questions 23-32 are based on the following passage.**

*This passage is adapted from Lynne Peeples "Moths Use Sonar-Jamming Defense to Fend Off Hunting Bats." © 2009 by Scientific American.*

An insect with paper-thin wings may carry much the same defense technology as some of the military's heavy-duty warships. The finding that a species of tiger moth can jam the sonar of echolocating bats to avoid being eaten
5  seems to be the "first conclusive evidence of sonar jamming in nature," says Aaron Corcoran, a biology PhD student at Wake Forest University and the lead author of the paper reporting the discovery. "It demonstrates a new level of escalation in the bat–moth evolutionary arms race."
10  Before Corcoran's study, scientists were puzzled by why certain species of tiger moths made sound. Some speculated that the moths use it to startle bats. A few pointed to its potential interference with their echolocation. General consensus, however, fell with a third hypothesis: clicks
15  function to warn a predator not to eat the clicking prey because it is toxic, or at least pretending to be.

To test these hypotheses, Corcoran and his team pitted the tiger moth *Bertholdia trigona* against the big brown bat *Eptesicus fuscus*, a battle frequently fought after
20  sundown from Central America to Colorado. High-speed infrared cameras and an ultrasonic microphone recorded the action over nine consecutive nights. The process of elimination began. If moth clicks served to startle, previous studies suggested the bats should become tolerant of the
25  sound within two or three days. "But that's not what we found," says Corcoran, explaining the lack of success bats had in capturing their clicking prey even through the last nights of the study.

How about the toxic warning theory? If this were the
30  case, according to Corcoran, bats would not find the moths palatable or, if they were indeed tasty, they would quickly learn they'd been tricked. Either way, bats should start to ignore the moth's unique ultrasonic clicks. Also, bats partook readily when offered *B. trigona* that lacked the
35  ability to click, and they kept coming back for more. This attraction also held true for clicking *B. trigona*: The predators persisted after their prey despite only reaching them about 20 percent of the time. Bats actually launched four times as many successful attacks against a control group
40  of silent moths. These findings are "only consistent with the jamming hypothesis," Corcoran notes. "But the most distinctive evidence was in the echolocation sequences of the bats."

Normally, a bat attack starts with relatively intermittent
45  sounds. They then increase in frequency—up to 200 cries per second—as the bat gets closer to the moth "so it knows where the moth is at that critical moment," Corcoran explains. But his research showed that just as bats were increasing their click frequency, moths "turn on sound
50  production full blast," clicking at a rate of up to 4,500 times a second. This furious clicking by the moths reversed the bats' pattern—the frequency of bat sonar decreased, rather than increased, as it approached its prey, suggesting that it lost its target.
55  The biological mechanism behind the moth's defense strategy is still unclear to researchers. "Most likely, moth clicks are disrupting the bat's neural processing of when echoes return," Corcoran says. Bats judge how far away a moth is based on the time delay between making the cry and
60  its audible return. This "blurring" of the bat's vision, he explains, "may be just enough to keep the moth safe."

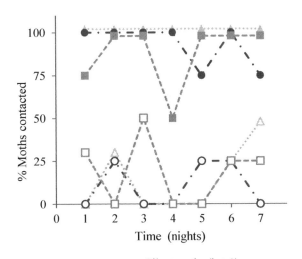

Bat Attack Success Rates

········▲········ Silent moths (bat 1)
— ●— Silent moths (bat 2)
–●– Silent moths (bat 3)
········△········ Clicking moths (bat 1)
— ○— Clicking moths (bat 2)
–□– Clicking moths (bat 3)

**GO ON TO THE NEXT PAGE**

23. The passage is primarily concerned with

    (A) the ways *Eptesicus fuscus* bats capture moths.
    (B) the discovery that tiger moths can jam bats' sonar.
    (C) how the tiger moths' clicking defense works.
    (D) why tiger moths developed defenses against bats.

24. The author describes alternate hypotheses of the moths' clicking defense in order to

    (A) support her claim that researchers need more evidence before they can draw any conclusions.
    (B) show how the researchers' experiment disproved all but one of these hypotheses.
    (C) signal to the reader that the researchers' data shows only one side of the debate.
    (D) explain the multiple reasons that this defense is effective for the moths.

25. According to Aaron Corcoran's research, which of the following represents the tiger moths' most effective defensive countermeasure?

    (A) Poisonous bodies
    (B) Defensive maneuvering
    (C) Clicking ultrasonically
    (D) Hearing ability

26. Which choice provides the best evidence for the answer to the previous question?

    (A) Lines 3-8 ("The finding ... discovery")
    (B) Lines 13-16 ("General consensus ... be")
    (C) Lines 23-25 ("If moth ... days")
    (D) Lines 38-40 ("Bats actually ... moths")

27. According to the passage, the bats would not attack some tiger moths because

    (A) they lost "sight" of the moths via sonar when pursuing them.
    (B) they realized the moths were toxic after a few nights.
    (C) they preferred to focus their attention on easier prey.
    (D) the moths' ultrasonic clicks startled them, frightening them away.

28. Which choice provides the best evidence for the answer to the previous question?

    (A) Lines 11-12 ("Some speculated ... bats")
    (B) Lines 29-32 ("If this ... tricked")
    (C) Lines 51-54 ("This furious ... target")
    (D) Lines 58-60 ("Bats judge ... return")

29. As used in line 34, "partook readily" most nearly means

    (A) consumed without difficulty.
    (B) ate without hesitation.
    (C) shared happily.
    (D) participated promptly.

30. As used in line 44, "intermittent" most nearly means

    (A) random.
    (B) sporadic.
    (C) alternating.
    (D) scattered.

31. The passage discusses all of the following EXCEPT

    (A) the moths' effectiveness in warding off attacks from their predators.
    (B) whether these particular species would encounter one another in nature.
    (C) the lessons that can be learned by engineers from the moth's natural sonar jamming.
    (D) the bats' responses to moths that lacked the ability to click.

32. Information from the graph best supports which of the following statements?

    (A) Bats were more effective at hunting silent moths at end of the study than they were at the start.
    (B) Bats devoured half as many clicking moths as they did silent moths.
    (C) Bats became increasingly effective at hunting clicking moths with each subsequent night.
    (D) Silent moths were consistently more likely to be captured than clicking moths.

**GO ON TO THE NEXT PAGE**

**Questions 33-42 are based on the following passage.**

*The following passage is adapted from the story "The Godchildren," by Tessa Hadley, first published in The New Yorker in 2009.*

The three heirs, in three separate taxis, converged on 33 Everdene Walk on a fine afternoon in late May. They were in their early fifties, and had not met since they were sixteen or seventeen. Amanda, who had been officious even as a
5  teenager, had organized the meeting by e-mail, via the solicitors: "If we're all going to the house, why don't we go at the same time? Wouldn't it be fun to meet up?"

Now each was regretting having agreed to this.

Chris, who was a lecturer at a new university, was certain
10  that he had spotted Amanda at the station, ahead of him in the queue for taxis; he had been too embarrassed to make himself known to her, even though they could have shared the fare. She surely hadn't had all that red hair thirty-five years ago, and she hadn't seemed so tall then, or so loosely
15  put together: the woman in the queue wasn't large, exactly, but physically complicated, with a bright-colored striped wrap tossed over one shoulder which made him think of beachwear. Perhaps she lived in a hot country. He'd recognized her only when she threw her unguarded, emphatic
20  glance at everyone behind her in the queue—boldly but blindly. Quailing, Chris was suddenly his anguished seventeen-year-old self again, stripped of his disguise as someone experienced and distinguished.

His memories of Mandy, young, were dim but had an
25  ominous intensity. He wished he hadn't come. He knew already that he wouldn't want anything, anyway, from the horrible old house. At least he wouldn't be alone with Amanda; although when he tried to recover his memories of Susan, the other godchild, he couldn't find anything at all,
30  only a neatly labeled vacancy.

The three taxis bore them, just a few minutes apart, out of the city center, then, swooping decorously downhill between traffic lights, through a species of suburb that seemed more remote from their present lives than anywhere they ever went
35  on holiday.

By the time these three had come, as children, to visit their godmother here, their more fashionable parents had already decided that the suburbs were dreary: places to joke about, not to aspire to. Their parents were doing up, in those
40  days, spindly dilapidated eighteenth-century houses, bought cheap, in the city center. Susan's mother still lived in one of these, now worth a great deal, and Susan had spent the previous night in her childhood bed. In her taxi, she was hardly thinking of the meeting ahead—except to wish that

45  she weren't going to it. She was obsessing over jagged old irritations, roused by a conversation with her mother that morning.

Chris's and Susan's taxis pulled up outside 33 Everdene Walk at the same moment; Amanda had got there before
50  them, and the front door stood open to what seemed, to their foreboding, a seething blackness, in contrast to the glare outside. Who knew what state the house would be in? Susan was quicker, paying her taxi off; Chris was always afraid that he would tip too little or too much. She looked away while
55  he probed in his change purse, then they politely pretended to recognize each other. He tried to dig back in his mind to their old acquaintance: how hadn't he seen that the invisible, unremembered Susan might grow into this slim, long-faced, long-legged dark woman, somewhat ravaged but contained
60  and elegant?

Meanwhile, Amanda, watching from a window she had just opened upstairs, saw thirty-five years of change heaped in one awful moment on both their heads. They looked broken-down to her, appalling. On her way to the house, she
65  had bullied her resisting taxi-driver into two consecutive U-turns between the lime trees: visited by a premonition of just this disappointment, and then recovering, repressing her dread, willing herself to hope. Amanda remembered the old days more vividly than either of the others, cherished the
70  idea of their shared past—strangely, because at the time she had seemed the one most ready to trample it underfoot, on her way to better things. Now she revolted at Chris's untidy gray-white locks, windswept without wind, around his bald patch: why did men yield so readily to their disintegration?
75  At least Susan had the decency to keep her hair brown and well cut. Chris was stooping and bobbing at Susan, smiling lopsidedly, self-deprecatory.

She whistled from the window, piercing the Walk's tranquility.
80  "Come on up!" she shouted. "Prepare for the Chamber of Horrors!"

33. Amanda, Susan, and Chris are meeting up because

(A) their father died and they need to discuss his will.
(B) they wanted to have a reunion after thirty-five years, since they had once been great friends.
(C) they are going to an open house that is in a desirable neighborhood.
(D) their godmother passed away and they need to sort through her belongings.

**GO ON TO THE NEXT PAGE**

34. Based on the information in the passage, Chris's memories of the other two godchildren

    (A) perfectly matched his impressions of them later on.
    (B) were colored negatively by his subsequent interactions with them.
    (C) were almost non-existent, as he had forgotten all about them over the years.
    (D) seemed inadequate and incomplete when confronted with the women in-person.

35. In the passage, Amanda, Chris, and Susan all experience the greatest sense of foreboding about

    (A) seeing one another again after all these years.
    (B) entering the dilapidated, potentially unsafe house.
    (C) confronting the memories of their dead godparent.
    (D) whether they'll receive the fair portion of their inheritance.

36. Which choice provides the best evidence for the answer to the previous question?

    (A) Lines 2-4 ("They were ... seventeen")
    (B) Line 8 ("Now each ... this")
    (C) Lines 25-27 ("He knew ... house")
    (D) Lines 80-81 ("Prepare for ... Horrors")

37. The passage hints that Chris

    (A) has an unresolved history with Amanda.
    (B) used to be in love with Susan.
    (C) is a reformed rebel.
    (D) was always their godparent's favorite.

38. Which choice provides the best evidence for the answer to the previous question?

    (A) Lines 18-21 ("He'd recognized ... blindly")
    (B) Lines 24-25 ("His memories ... intensity")
    (C) Lines 56-60 ("He tried ... elegant")
    (D) Lines 72-74 ("Now she ... disintegration")

39. As used in line 4, "officious" most nearly means

    (A) presumptuous.
    (B) busy.
    (C) pushy.
    (D) informal.

40. The rhetorical effect of the phrase "a neatly labeled vacancy" (line 30) is to suggest that

    (A) Chris had intentionally suppressed painful memories about Susan.
    (B) Chris often had difficulties in recalling his childhood.
    (C) Chris had no strong memories of one of his fellow godchildren.
    (D) Susan had been so dull in her youth that few people remembered her.

41. As used in line 46, "roused" most nearly means

    (A) provoked.
    (B) stimulated.
    (C) excited.
    (D) galvanized.

42. How does Amanda's assessment of her two old acquaintances compare with Chris's assessment?

    (A) Chris was delighted to see the other two, while Amanda was annoyed.
    (B) Chris was surprised at the changes in his acquaintances, while Amanda was disappointed in them.
    (C) Chris thought the two women looked overdressed, while Amanda thought the others should have put more effort into their appearance.
    (D) Chris thought the other two looked old, while Amanda thought they looked surprisingly good for their age.

**GO ON TO THE NEXT PAGE**

**Questions 43-52 are based on the following passage.**

*President Richard Nixon resigned his office on August 9, 1974. His decision followed the revelation that five men connected to the Nixon administration were caught breaking into the headquarters of the opposing political party. At the time of Nixon's resignation, proceedings had already begun in Congress to impeach him and seemed likely to succeed.*

Good evening. This is the 37th time I have spoken to you from this office, where so many decisions have been made that shaped the history of this Nation. Each time I have done so to discuss with you some matter that I believe affected the
5    national interest. Throughout the long and difficult period of Watergate, I have felt it was my duty to persevere—to make every possible effort to complete the term of office to which you elected me. In the past few days, however, it has become evident to me that I no longer have a strong enough political
10   base in the Congress to justify continuing that effort. As long as there was such a base, I felt strongly that it was necessary to see the constitutional process through to its conclusion; that to do otherwise would be unfaithful to the spirit of that deliberately difficult process, and a dangerously destabilizing
15   precedent for the future. But with the disappearance of that base, I now believe that the constitutional purpose has been served. And there is no longer a need for the process to be prolonged.

I would have preferred to carry through to the finish,
20   whatever the personal agony it would have involved, and my family unanimously urged me to do so. But the interests of the nation must always come before any personal considerations. From the discussions I have had with Congressional and other leaders I have concluded that
25   because of the Watergate matter I might not have the support of the Congress that I would consider necessary to back the very difficult decisions and carry out the duties of this office in the way the interests of the nation will require.

I have never been a quitter. To leave office before my
30   term is completed is abhorrent to every instinct in my body. But as President, I must put the interests of America first. America needs a full-time President and a full-time Congress, particularly at this time with problems we face at home and abroad. To continue to fight through the months
35   ahead for my personal vindication would almost totally absorb the time and attention of both the President and the Congress in a period when our entire focus should be on the great issues of peace abroad and prosperity without inflation at home. Therefore, I shall resign the Presidency effective at
40   noon tomorrow. Vice President Ford will be sworn in as President at that hour in this office.

By taking this action, I hope that I will have hastened the start of that process of healing which is so desperately
45   needed in America. I regret deeply any injuries that may have been done in the course of the events that led to this decision. I would say only that if some of my Judgments were wrong, and some were wrong, they were made in what I believed at the time to be the best interest of the Nation.
50   As I recall the high hopes for America with which we began this second term, I feel a great sadness that I will not be here in this office working on your behalf to achieve those hopes in the next two and a half years. But in turning over direction of the Government to Vice President Ford, I know,
55   as I told the nation when I nominated him for that office ten months ago, that the leadership of America would be in good hands.

So let us all now join together in affirming that common commitment and in helping our new President succeed for
60   the benefit of all Americans. I shall leave this office with regret at not completing my term but with gratitude for the privilege of serving as your President for the past five and a half years. These years have been a momentous time in the history of our nation and the world. They have been a time of
65   achievement in which we can all be proud, achievements that represent the shared efforts of the administration, the Congress and the people. But the challenges ahead are equally great. And they, too, will require the support and the efforts of the Congress and the people, working in
70   cooperation with the new Administration.

May God's grace be with you in all the days ahead.

43. Nixon's primary purpose in delivering this speech was most likely to

(A) ask the American public for their forgiveness for his mistakes.
(B) announce his resignation and offer an explanation to the public.
(C) condemn the press for trying him in the court of public opinion before all the facts were available.
(D) express his full confidence in Vice President Ford.

GO ON TO THE NEXT PAGE

**44.** Which choice provides the best evidence for the answer to the previous question?

(A) Lines 5-8 ("Throughout the ... me")
(B) Line 31 ("But as ... first")
(C) Lines 34-38 ("To continue ... home")
(D) Lines 40-41 ("Vice President ... office")

**45.** Nixon's tone in the passage can best be described as

(A) regretful.
(B) hopeful.
(C) livid.
(D) uncertain.

**46.** Which of the following is NOT a reason Nixon gives for resigning the presidency?

(A) He no longer feels he has enough congressional support.
(B) He can't fulfill his obligations as President while also fighting for his personal vindication in the Watergate scandal.
(C) Vice President Ford stated he was ready to take on the duties of the presidency.
(D) The United States faces great challenges in the coming years and requires a cooperative government to face them.

**47.** The passage implies that Nixon

(A) wanted to continue in his office, but felt obligated to resign.
(B) was in fact relieved to step aside.
(C) resigned in order to spend more time with his family.
(D) was blackmailed into resigning by Congress.

**48.** Which choice provides the best evidence for the answer to the previous question?

(A) Lines 1-3 ("This is ... nation")
(B) Lines 21-23 ("But the ... considerations")
(C) Lines 52-56 ("But in ... hands")
(D) Lines 59-62 ("I shall ... years")

**49.** Nixon's use of the phrase "dangerously destabilizing precedent for the future" (lines 14-15) is primarily meant to refer to

(A) forcing congress to initiate impeachment proceedings.
(B) permitting the president's party to get away with crimes.
(C) resigning too easily while he still had political support.
(D) finishing out his term in the face of serious accusations.

**50.** Which of the following is an issue that Nixon states Americans must address in the coming years?

(A) A potential economic collapse
(B) An overly powerful Congress
(C) A trial of those involved in Watergate
(D) A struggle for peace

**51.** As used in line 30, "abhorrent" most nearly means

(A) pitiful.
(B) shocking.
(C) disgusting.
(D) repugnant.

**52.** As used in line 57, "affirming" most nearly means

(A) stating.
(B) defending.
(C) upholding.
(D) swearing.

# STOP

**If you complete the problem set before time elapses, you may review your responses for this section.**

**Do not view or begin working on any other sections.**

## Acknowledgements for this Section

The passages in section 1 were adapted from the following sources:

1. Atul Grover, Elliot S. Fisher, "Should Hospital Residency Programs Be Expanded to Increase the Number of Doctors?" © *The Wall Street Journal*, originally published June 16th, 2013.

2. Chensheng (Alex) Lu, Janet H. Silverstein, "Would Americans Be Better Off Eating a Mostly Organic Diet?" © *The Wall Street Journal*, originally published June 16th, 2013.

3. Lynne Peeples, "Moths Use Sonar-Jamming Defense to Fend Off Hunting Bats." © *Scientific American*, originally published July 16th, 2009.

4. Tessa Hadley, "The Godchildren." Originally published in *The New Yorker*, October 12th, 2009.

5. Richard Nixon, Farewell Address. Delivered on August 8th, 1974.

# Section 2

## SECTION 2
### Time – 25 minutes
### 20 Questions

Turn to Section 2 of your answer sheet to answer the questions in this section.

**Notes**

1. Choose the best answer choice of those provided. Be sure to fill in the corresponding circle on your answer sheet.
2. You may NOT use a calculator on this section.
3. If a problem includes a figure and does not state that the figure is NOT to scale, you may assume the figure provides a correct representation of the information in the problem.
4. The domain of any function $f$ is the set of all real numbers $x$ for which $f(x)$ is a real number, unless otherwise stated.

**Reference**

$A = \frac{1}{2}bh$

$a^2 + b^2 = c^2$

Special Triangles

$V = \frac{1}{3}lwh$

$V = \frac{1}{3}\pi r^2 h$

$A = lw$

$V = lwh$

$V = \pi r^2 h$

$A = \pi r^2$

$C = 2\pi r$

$V = \frac{4}{3}\pi r^3$

There are 360° in a circle.

The sum of the angles in a triangle is 180°.

The number of radians of arc in a circle is $2\pi$.

GO ON TO THE NEXT PAGE

1. If $42 = 3(x - 4)$, what is the value of $x$?

    (A)  4
    (B) 10
    (C) 18
    (D) 20

2. For what value of $k$ does $x^2 + kx + 9 = (x + 3)^2$?

    (A) 0
    (B) 3
    (C) 6
    (D) 9

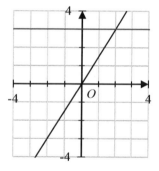

3. If $(x, y)$ is the solution to the system of equations graphed above, what is the value of $x$ in terms of $y$?

    (A) $y$

    (B) $\dfrac{2}{3}y$

    (C) $\dfrac{1}{3}y$

    (D) $-\dfrac{1}{3}y$

4. A barrel of crude oil is extracted from shale at a cost of \$51, and then transported to and from the refinery at a cost of \$6 each direction. Oil is processed three times at the refinery plant, at a cost of \$9 each time. What is the profit, in dollars per barrel, if one barrel is sold for \$93? (Profit is equal to revenue minus expenses.)

    (A) 1
    (B) 2
    (C) 3
    (D) 4

5. If $c - 1 = 3$, what is the value of $c^2 - 1$?

    (A)  3
    (B)  8
    (C) 10
    (D) 15

**GO ON TO THE NEXT PAGE**

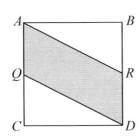

**6.** The square above has an area of 100. If $Q$ is the midpoint of $\overline{AC}$ and $R$ is the midpoint of $\overline{BD}$, what is the area of the shaded area?

(A) 40
(B) 50
(C) 60
(D) 75

**7.** If $2(3a - b) = 4b$ and $b = 6$, what is the value of $a$?

(A)  6
(B) –6
(C)  2
(D)  5

$$\frac{2x}{x-1} - \frac{3x}{x+1}$$

**8.** Which of the following expressions is equivalent to the expression above?

(A) $-\dfrac{x}{x^2 - 1}$

(B) $\dfrac{5x - x^2}{x^2 - 1}$

(C) $-\dfrac{x}{x - 1}$

(D) $-\dfrac{6x}{x^2 - 1}$

**9.** Joel is $a$ years older than Luca. In $b$ years, Joel will be twice as old as Luca. What is Joel's present age, in terms of $a$ and $b$?

(A) $-2(a - b)$
(B) $-2a - b$
(C) $2a - b$
(D) $a - b$

$$|x - 3| \le 5$$

**10.** Which of the following inequalities is equivalent to the absolute value inequality above?

(A) $-2 \le x \le 8$
(B) $-8 \le x \le 2$
(C) $x \le -2$ or $x \ge 8$
(D) $x \le -8$ or $x \ge 2$

**GO ON TO THE NEXT PAGE** ⇨

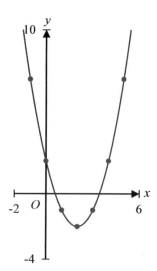

**11.** The figure above shows the graph of a quadratic function $f$ with a minimum point at $(2,-2)$. If $f(5) = n$, what is a possible value for $n$?

(A) $f(-2)$
(B) $f(-1)$
(C) $f(0)$
(D) $f(1)$

$$\frac{16^x}{4^a + 4^a + 4^a + 4^a} = \frac{1}{4}$$

**12.** Which equation best represents the value of $x$ in terms of $a$?

(A) $\dfrac{a}{4} = x$

(B) $\dfrac{a}{2} = x$

(C) $a = x$

(D) $2a = x$

**13.** The sum of $a$ and $b$ is 132. If $a$ is the square of $b$ and the product of $a$ and $b$ is negative, what is $a$?

(A) $-12$
(B) 11
(C) 121
(D) 144

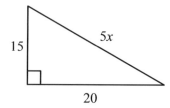

**14.** What is the value of $x$ in the triangle above?

(A) 5
(B) 10
(C) 25
(D) 31

$$y = 5x^2 - 3x - 1$$

$$y + 6 = 7x$$

**15.** In the system of equations above, what is the value of $y$ in terms of $x$?

(A) $-x$
(B) $x$
(C) $2x$
(D) $3x$

**GO ON TO THE NEXT PAGE**

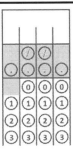
**Directions:** For questions 16-20, fill out your answers using the grids in Section 2 of your answer sheet.

You will need to enter your answers for the following questions in the grids provided in your answer sheet.

- Make sure to fill in bubbles completely.
- Mark no more than one circle in any column.
- Answers written in the boxes above the grid are *not* scored.
- You can write your answer into those boxes as a guide when you bubble in your answers, however, remember that you always need to bubble your answers as well!

**Placement:**

You can start your answer in any column as long as you can fit in the whole answer.

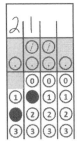 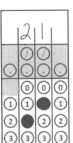 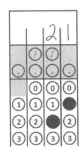

**Reminders:**

- Some grid-in problems have more than one correct answer. In those cases, you may grid in any of the possible answers as long as it fits in the grid.
- If you get a decimal answer with more digits than can fit in the grid, round your answer but make sure that it fills the entire grid.

**Mixed Numbers:**

There is no negative sign in the grid, so all answers will be positive numbers or zero. You can grid proper and improper fractions, but *not* mixed numbers. For example, the mixed number $3\frac{1}{4}$ must be written as 13/4 or 3.25. If you grid the answer as the mixed number 31/4, the machine will read it as $\frac{31}{4}$, which is incorrect.

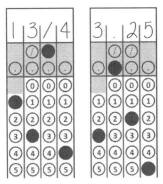

GO ON TO THE NEXT PAGE ▶

Unapproved reproduction or distribution of any portion of this material is unlawful.

16. A stone is dropped from a height of 9 meters above the ground. If the height function can be modelled by the equation $h(t) = a - t^2$, where $t$ is time in seconds and $h$ is height in meters, how many seconds does it take for the stone to hit the ground?

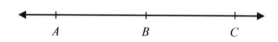

$$A \qquad B \qquad C$$

17. $A$, $B$ and $C$ lie on a line, as shown above. The length of $\overline{AB}$ is $x - 4$ and the length of $\overline{AC}$ is $x + 6$. What is the length of $\overline{BC}$?

18. If $f(x) = 8x + 1$ and $g(x) = 3x - 1$, what is the value of $\dfrac{f(2)}{g(f(0))}$?

$$\frac{d}{y} = \frac{12}{d}$$

$$y^2 = 6y - 9$$

19. If $d$ is positive, what is the value of $d$ in the series of equations above?

20. The imaginary number $i$ is defined such that $i^2 = -1$. What is the value of $(1 - i\sqrt{5})(1 + i\sqrt{5})$?

# STOP

**If you complete the problem set before time elapses, you may review your responses for this section.**

**Do not view or begin working on any other sections.**

# Section 3

Unapproved reproduction or distribution of any portion of this material is unlawful.

## SECTION 3
### Time – 35 minutes
### 44 Questions

Turn to Section 3 of your answer sheet to answer the questions in this section.

**Directions:** For these questions, determine the solution to each question presented and choose the best answer choices of those provided. Be sure to fill in the respective circle on your answer sheet.

**Questions 1-11 are based on the following passage.**

**A Marine Biologist's Day in Maine**

Lucy is up by eight in the morning. ◼ <u>By nine, she's out the door.</u> She'll be on the beach by nine thirty, but Lucy isn't headed out to tan; Lucy is a marine biologist. She got her PhD last year, and she's now doing post-doctorate research on the coast of Maine.

[1] She meets the other researchers out by the tide pools. [2] They're focused this month on the effects of an ◼ <u>intrusive</u> green crab population that has been harming the balance of the coastal ecosystem. [3] This loss of clams affects other species as well as the economy: the Maine clam industry typically makes $17 million annually, and the lost profits will affect fishermen, distributors, and consumers. [4] ◼ <u>The crabs eat soft-shell clams and as a result the clam population is plummeting, and clams are invertebrates.</u> [5] Today, the research team will gather samples of both crabs and clams. ◼

1. (A) NO CHANGE
   (B) Lucy goes out the door after that.
   (C) Then she just walks out the door.
   (D) It's 9:00 o'clock when she leaves.

2. (A) NO CHANGE
   (B) encroaching
   (C) invasive
   (D) infringing

3. Which choice best improves or maintains the focus of the paragraph?

   (A) NO CHANGE
   (B) The crabs eat soft-shell clams and as a result the clam population is plummeting.
   (C) The crabs eat soft-shell clams, and clams are invertebrates.
   (D) Soft-shell clams are invertebrates, and their population is plummeting as they are eaten by crabs.

4. To make this paragraph most logical, sentence [3] should be placed

   (A) Where it is now
   (B) Before sentence 1
   (C) After sentence 4
   (D) After sentence 5

GO ON TO THE NEXT PAGE

3 3

Unapproved reproduction or distribution
of any portion of this material is unlawful.

Arriving at the work **5** cite, Lucy feels a misty spray on her arms as breakers crash on the rocks. The air is chilly; it's early June but it still feels more like spring than summer. Lucy hears another researcher say, "I love everything about this job except having freezing fingers first thing in the morning." Plunging her hands into a tide pool, she can't help but disagree. **6** The cold is a welcome shock to the system, instantly making Lucy feel more alert and invigorated.

They spend the morning collecting specimens. Crabs scuttle around, and clams lie still in their respective buckets. The day gets warmer, and Lucy works up a sweat. Compared to sitting at a desk, **7** the animals are lively. By noon, Lucy and her colleagues are gathering up their specimens and equipment to head indoors. **8**

Lucy spends the afternoon entering and analyzing data on a computer, tagging crabs in preparation for an experiment the following day, and monitoring the results of an ongoing experiment that focuses on the birthrate of phytoplankton, which are the primary component of the soft-shell clam's diet. **9** After dinner and a phone call, the phone call being from her sister, she puts in some hours on a research paper. Tomorrow will again start with a trip to the field station, as they continue to examine the changing ecosystem's challenges.

5. (A) NO CHANGE
   (B) sight
   (C) sleight
   (D) site

6. The writer is considering deleting the underlined sentence. Should the sentence be kept or deleted?

   (A) Kept, because it helps to maintain a clear chronology of events in the story.
   (B) Kept, because it helps to explain why Lucy disagrees with the other researcher.
   (C) Deleted, because Lucy's opinions about cold water are not statements of fact.
   (D) Deleted, because it doesn't provide relevant information about the qualifications necessary to become a marine biologist.

7. (A) NO CHANGE
   (B) working with the animals is a lively activity.
   (C) the biologists are livelier.
   (D) the animal is lively.

8. The writer wants to insert another sentence here to wrap up the events of this paragraph, and provide an effective transition to the next. Which of the following choices best accomplishes these goals?

   (A) Lucy is sad to leave the shore, because working on the shore is her favorite part of the day.
   (B) After depositing their specimens in holding tanks, they have a quick break for lunch and then get to work in the lab.
   (C) They work quickly, because it's almost time for lunch and everyone has worked up an appetite collecting specimens.
   (D) The equipment will be stored for later use, and the specimens will be placed in holding tanks.

9. (A) NO CHANGE
   (B) After dinner, and also after a phone call from her sister, she works on putting in some hours on a research paper.
   (C) After dinner and a phone call from her sister, she works on a research paper.
   (D) After eating dinner and then speaking on the phone with her sister, she then works on doing some work for a research paper.

**GO ON TO THE NEXT PAGE**

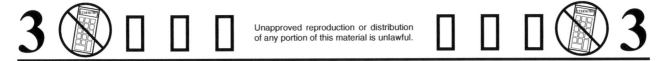

**10** When we hear about problems in the ocean, it's easy for us to think that we don't affect us. However, changes in ocean populations affect populations on land, as well as the economy. **11** Nobody are at the forefront of addressing these oceanic environmental concerns like marine biologists.

10. (A) NO CHANGE
    (B) When we hear about problems in the ocean, it's easy for them to think that they don't affect them.
    (C) When we hear about problems in the ocean, it's easy for us to think that they don't affect us.
    (D) When you hear about problems in the ocean, it's easy for us to think that they don't affect us.

11. (A) NO CHANGE
    (B) Nobody at the forefront
    (C) Somebody are at the forefront
    (D) Nobody is at the forefront

**GO ON TO THE NEXT PAGE**

Unapproved reproduction or distribution of any portion of this material is unlawful.

**Questions 12-22 are based on the following passage.**

**Comets, Briefly Brightening our Skies**

[12] Blazing through the sky for short periods of time before disappearing into the galaxy, humans have long been fascinated by comets. Comets are balls of dust and ice, comprised of leftover materials that did not become planets during the formation of our solar system.

[1] Comets travel around the sun in a highly elliptical orbit. [2] When far from the sun, a comet consists of only its nucleus, which is a few kilometers wide. [3] As the nucleus gets closer to the sun (about as close as Jupiter), some of its ice sublimates, or turns directly into gas without melting into liquid first. [4] The coma, a cloud of gas created by the process of sublimation, is very large compared to the initial size of the nucleus. [13] [5] Solar winds disrupt [14] rock particles dust, and gas, creating distinct tails of particles streaming out from the coma. [6] These tails can exceed 150 million kilometers in [15] length but are visible from Earth. [7] [16] Because tails are caused by solar winds, they are always moving away from the sun. [8] Thus, surprisingly, if a comet is moving away from the sun then it is following [17] it's tail. [9] Comets that are sublimating and have a tail are among the fastest objects in our solar system, reaching speeds up to 160,000 kilometers per hour.

12. (A) NO CHANGE
    (B) Before disappearing into the galaxy, humans have long been fascinated by comets, blazing through the sky for brief periods of time.
    (C) Comets, blazing through the sky for brief periods of time before disappearing into the galaxy, have long fascinated humans.
    (D) For brief periods of time, humans have long been fascinated by comets, blazing through the sky before disappearing into the galaxy.

13. The writer wants to insert a sentence here which will provide additional support for the preceding sentence. Which choice best accomplishes this goal?

    (A) On the surface of Mars, frozen CO2 sublimates in warmer months.
    (B) Comas vary in size, depending on the initial size of the nucleus and environmental factors.
    (C) The coma can reach up to 10,000 kilometers in diameter, which is close to the size of the planet Earth.
    (D) At least one comet's tail was longer than 320 million kilometers.

14. (A) NO CHANGE
    (B) rock particles, dust, and gas,
    (C) rock particles dust and gas
    (D) rock particles, dust, and, gas

15. (A) NO CHANGE
    (B) length, are
    (C) length and are
    (D) length, further are

16. Which choice most clearly explains why comet tails move away from the sun?

    (A) NO CHANGE
    (B) Tails, because of their cause, solar winds, are always moving away from the sun.
    (C) They are being caused by solar winds, and tails are always moving away from the sun.
    (D) Tails are always moving away from the sun, being caused by solar winds.

17. (A) NO CHANGE
    (B) it
    (C) its'
    (D) its

GO ON TO THE NEXT PAGE

The sun is near the center of Earth's orbit. However, a comet travels differently: the sun is at one of the far sides of its elliptical orbit. As the comet approaches the sun its velocity **18** increases, and as it moves farther away from the sun its velocity increases. Some comets **19** do an orbit around the sun in a few years, while others take thousands of years to do so.

Although it is a rare occurrence, sometimes **20** comets collide with another celestial body. A popular theory is that a comet first brought water to Earth. The last known collision on Earth was 65 million years ago, when a comet or an asteroid hit the Earth just south of the Yucatan peninsula, creating a massive crater. The impact caused a global dust cloud to rise which blocked the sun and cooled the entire planet.

**21** When Halley's Comet last neared the Earth in 1986, scientists determined that it is made up of carbon, hydrogen, oxygen, and nitrogen in proportions similar to those of the human body. As distant and as different as comets may seem from us as they trail across the sky, we are **22** composed of the same elements.

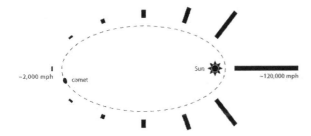

18. Which choice completes the sentence with accurate information based on the graphic?

   (A) NO CHANGE
   (B) increases as the length of its tail increases, which decreases as it moves away from the sun.
   (C) increases, and as it moves farther away from the sun its velocity decreases.
   (D) decreases, and as it moves closer to the sun the length of its tail decreases.

19. (A) NO CHANGE
    (B) make an orbit of
    (C) orbit
    (D) complete a whole entire orbit around

20. (A) NO CHANGE
    (B) comets collides with another celestial body.
    (C) a comet collides with other celestial bodies.
    (D) comets collide with other celestial bodies.

21. The writer is considering dividing the underlined sentence into two sentences. Should the underlined sentence be divided into two sentences?

   (A) Yes, because it is a run-on sentence.
   (B) Yes, because the sentence mixes unrelated pieces of information without explanation.
   (C) No, because the conjunction "and" effectively links the various ideas expressed in the sentence.
   (D) No, because the several pieces of information in the sentence serve to express a single complete thought.

22. (A) NO CHANGE
    (B) constituted with
    (C) arranged among
    (D) produced through

GO ON TO THE NEXT PAGE

Unapproved reproduction or distribution of any portion of this material is unlawful.

**Questions 23-33 are based on the following passage.**

**Hamilton's Essential Contributions to the United States' Economy**

[23] Of all the Founding Fathers, Alexander Hamilton's contributions to the establishment of the United States' economy were unparalleled. A trusted advisor of George Washington during the Revolutionary War, Hamilton spent a lot of time thinking about what kind of government the new country needed. He studied European economies and governments, and maintained that strong federal power was necessary for the nation's survival. [24] You may not know that when delegates convened in 1787 to create a Constitution for the new country, Hamilton was active at the Convention and instrumental in the Constitution's ratification. He convinced states to approve it through speeches and the influential Federalist Papers which he co-authored.

[1] [25] President Washington decided on the choice of Hamilton as the first Secretary of the Treasury. [2] Washington and his cabinet had no example to follow: they set the [26] preceding for how the executive branch of the government would operate. [3] Thus, Hamilton was largely responsible for establishing the United States' early economic policies. [4] Thomas Jefferson was influential as Secretary of State as well. [5] Without sound economic policies, the country might not have survived. [27]

23. (A) NO CHANGE
   (B) Even among those of all of the Founding Fathers, Alexander Hamilton's contributions to the establishment of the United States' economy
   (C) Alexander Hamilton's were the greatest, the contributions of all of the Founding Fathers
   (D) Alexander Hamilton, more than any other contributions to the establishment of the United States' economy,

24. (A) NO CHANGE
   (B) I have heard that when delegates convened
   (C) When delegates convened
   (D) Posterity remembers that when delegates convened

25. (A) NO CHANGE
   (B) President Washington made the choice to have Hamilton be the first Secretary
   (C) President Washington chose Hamilton to be the first Secretary
   (D) President Washington made his choice and decided on Hamilton as first Secretary

26. (A) NO CHANGE
   (B) precedent
   (C) proceeding
   (D) president

27. Which sentence should be removed in order to improve the focus of this paragraph?

   (A) Sentence 1
   (B) Sentence 2
   (C) Sentence 3
   (D) Sentence 4

**GO ON TO THE NEXT PAGE**

Practice Test 1

Unapproved reproduction or distribution
of any portion of this material is unlawful.

**28** Hamilton knew the United States needed to have strong businesses and industries, which could not form without a strong national economy. The country was still deep in debt from the war and needed additional revenue to initiate national projects. Although taxes were **29** unpopular—a major cause of the Revolutionary War was American resentment toward British taxes, Hamilton argued for their necessity. Without capital, how could the government accomplish anything?

**30** Hamilton's "Report on Credit" stated that the government needed to repay its war bonds, take on the war debts of the states, and place a tax on imported goods. Many **31** members of Congress thought covering states' war debts expanded the central government's power too much, but Hamilton pointed out the difficulties of each state doing so independently. Virginia was strongly opposed to Hamilton's proposal, so Hamilton met secretly with Virginia Congressman James Madison. They agreed that Virginia would support the measure if the nation's new capital would be just outside Virginia, rather than in New York. With Virginia's support, the measures of the "Report on Credit" passed.

Another of Hamilton's ideas that met **32** obstacles was a national bank. Again, many states thought a federal bank would place too much power in the hands of the central **33** government and so for the sake of efficiency, and to establish credit for the federal government, the nation needed a centralized bank. In 1790, the idea was approved.

By influencing the Constitution's content and ensuring its ratification, and by developing the economic practices of the nascent government and establishing the national bank, Alexander Hamilton was the most influential economic developer of the young United States of America.

28. (A) NO CHANGE
    (B) Hamilton knew; the United States
    (C) Hamilton knew, the United States
    (D) Hamilton, knew the United States,

29. (A) NO CHANGE
    (B) unpopular, a major cause of the Revolutionary War was American resentment toward British taxes; Hamilton
    (C) unpopular, a major cause of the Revolutionary War was American resentment toward British taxes— Hamilton
    (D) unpopular—a major cause of the Revolutionary War was American resentment toward British taxes— Hamilton

30. Which choice most effectively establishes the main topic of the paragraph?
    (A) Virginians and New Yorkers wanted the nation's capital to be in their respective states.
    (B) On January 14, 1790, Hamilton presented Congress with a plan of action for jumpstarting the economy.
    (C) President Washington relied on Hamilton.
    (D) Hamilton threw himself into his work, becoming increasingly obsessive as he developed his plans.

31. (A) NO CHANGE
    (B) members' of Congress thought covering states war debts
    (C) members of Congress thought covering state's war debts
    (D) members of Congress thought covering states war debts

32. (A) NO CHANGE
    (B) resistance
    (C) problems
    (D) hardships

33. (A) NO CHANGE
    (B) government. However,
    (C) government and however,
    (D) government. Thus,

**GO ON TO THE NEXT PAGE**

**Questions 34-44 are based on the following passage.**

**Artistic Game Changer: Marcel Duchamp**

The twentieth century saw a major expansion of the definition of "art." Though visual art developed and flourished in practically every culture worldwide for millennia before the twentieth century, most schools of art had emphasized formal elements and aesthetics. The modern art movement, which began in the second half of the nineteenth century, had already [34] lengthened the scope of what the public accepted as art. Rather than aiming to represent their subjects directly, modern artists experimented with color and form to produce striking visual effects. By challenging the public's expectations for visual art, they laid the groundwork for the conceptual [35] art movement. Conceptual artists shifted the focus even further, from visual effects to ideas. They rejected the notion that a piece of art must be beautiful, or that it should demonstrate artistic skill—proclaiming, [36] rather, that as long as it expresses, an artistic concept, it should be considered art. Marcel Duchamp was a pioneer of the Conceptual art movement.

[1] Duchamp was born in France in 1887, [37] and by young adulthood it is true that he had spent time creating art in both France and the United States. [2] Many critics claimed that the piece was not legitimate, but he maintained that it was the provocative, innovative nature of his act that made it art. [3] Disenchanted with the commercial art world, he refused to engage in practices generally seen as necessary for financial success and recognition: developing an identifiable aesthetic, frequently showing his work publicly, [38] or creating pieces similar to each other for the sake of profit, and in 1955 he became a U.S. citizen. [4] He developed the notion of a "Readymade," a pre-existing object that an artist finds, chooses, and claims as art, [39] modifying the object only by signing it. [5] Famously, Duchamp's 1917 submission to an art exhibition, Fountain, consisted of a urinal that he rotated ninety degrees and signed with a pseudonym. [40]

34. (A) NO CHANGE
    (B) expanded
    (C) built
    (D) deepened

35. (A) NO CHANGE
    (B) art movement—Conceptual artists
    (C) art movement, conceptual artists
    (D) art movement: and conceptual artists

36. (A) NO CHANGE
    (B) rather: that as long as it expresses, an artistic concept, it should
    (C) rather, that as long as it expresses an artistic concept it should
    (D) rather that as long as it expresses an artistic concept it should

37. (A) NO CHANGE
    (B) and had spent time creating, by young adulthood, art
    (C) and created art, which by young adulthood he had spent time creating
    (D) and by young adulthood had spent time creating art

38. Which of the following choices most improves the focus of the passage?

    (A) or creating profits and becoming a citizen.
    (B) and in 1955 he became a U.S. citizen.
    (C) or creating pieces similar to each other for the sake of profit.
    (D) or creating pieces similar to each other for the sake of profit, and he became a U.S. citizen.

39. (A) NO CHANGE
    (B) modifying the object only by signing it by the artist.
    (C) modifying the object, the piece of art, only by signing it.
    (D) modifying the object only by applying his or her, the artist's, signature.

40. To make the paragraph most logical, sentence 2 should be placed

    (A) where it is now
    (B) before sentence 1
    (C) before sentence 5
    (D) after sentence 5

**GO ON TO THE NEXT PAGE**

In an interview in 1955, Duchamp **41** says, "You should wait for fifty . . . or a hundred years for your true public. That is the only public that interests me." **42** Because he did not receive critical acclaim for much of his career, over fifty years later Duchamp is seen as one of the most influential artists of the twentieth century. Duchamp's influence can be seen in the work of later conceptual artists: Andy Warhol, with his pop art images and prints of everyday objects; Jackson Pollock, with his canvases covered in splattered paint; Sol LeWitt, **43** who made cubic steel "structures." Thus, Duchamp achieved the respect of the public he cared **44** about! Duchamp and the conceptual art movement permanently changed ideas about art's definition, its scope, and its possibilities.

41. (A) NO CHANGE
    (B) was saying
    (C) is saying
    (D) said

42. (A) NO CHANGE
    (B) Considering that
    (C) Although
    (D) However

43. (A) NO CHANGE
    (B) with his
    (C) in making
    (D) by making

44. (A) NO CHANGE
    (B) about. Duchamp
    (C) about—Duchamp
    (D) about? Duchamp

# STOP

**If you complete the problem set before time elapses, you may review your responses for this section.**

**Do not view or begin working on any other sections.**

# Section 4

# SECTION 4
## Time – 55 minutes
## 38 Questions

---

**Turn to Section 4 of your answer sheet to answer the questions in this section.**

---

**Notes**

1. Choose the best answer choice of those provided. Be sure to fill in the corresponding circle on your answer sheet.

2. You may use a calculator on this section.

3. If a problem includes a figure and does not state that the figure is NOT to scale, you may assume the figure provides a correct representation of the information in the problem.

4. The domain of any function $f$ is the set of all real numbers $x$ for which $f(x)$ is a real number, unless otherwise stated.

---

**Reference**

$A = \frac{1}{2}bh$     $a^2 + b^2 = c^2$     Special Triangles     $V = \frac{1}{3}lwh$     $V = \frac{1}{3}\pi r^2 h$

$A = lw$     $V = lwh$     $V = \pi r^2 h$     $A = \pi r^2$     $V = \frac{4}{3}\pi r^3$

                                                                          $C = 2\pi r$

There are 360° in a circle.

The sum of the angles in a triangle is 180°.

The number of radians of arc in a circle is $2\pi$.

---

**GO ON TO THE NEXT PAGE**

1. If $y = x - 2$, and $x = 2y + 4$, what is the value of $x$?

   (A) 1
   (B) 0
   (C) –2
   (D) –6

3. If a farmer in Kansas purchases 8 pigs for every 1.5 acres of land, and has 6 acres of land set aside for pigs, how many pigs will she purchase?

   (A) 20
   (B) 32
   (C) 40
   (D) 48

$$\frac{x-1}{3} = \frac{2x-6}{4}$$

4. What is the value of $x$ that satisfies the equation above?

   (A) 5
   (B) 7
   (C) 8
   (D) 16

| $x$ | 0 | 2 | 4 | 6 |
|------|---|---|---|---|
| $f(x)$ | 3 | 4 | 5 | 6 |

2. Which of the following expressions defines $f(x)$ in the table above?

   (A) $f(x) = x + 3$
   (B) $f(x) = \frac{1}{2}x + 3$
   (C) $f(x) = x$
   (D) $f(x) = 2x$

5. If $8x + 4 = 48$, what is $2x + 1$?

   (A) 9
   (B) 10
   (C) 11
   (D) 12

GO ON TO THE NEXT PAGE

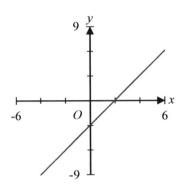

**6.** What is the slope of the function in the graph above?

(A) 2

(B) $\dfrac{3}{2}$

(C) $\dfrac{2}{3}$

(D) $\dfrac{1}{2}$

**7.** The population of an invasive species of moth doubles every 5 years. If the initial population is 300, what will be the population after 15 years?

(A)  900
(B) 1200
(C) 2000
(D) 2400

**8.** John fills his bag with five cent candies, $v$, and ten cent candies, $t$. If he has a total of 54 candies and his candies are worth \$3.10, which of the following is true?

    I.   $\$0.05v + \$0.10t = \$3.10$

    II.  $54 = v + t$

    III. $\$0.05 \times (54 - v) + \$0.10v = \$3.10$

(A) I only
(B) I and II only
(C) I, II, and III
(D) None of the above

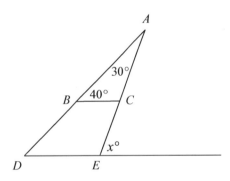

**9.** In the figure above, if $\overline{BC} \parallel \overline{DE}$, what is the value of $x$?

(A)  30
(B)  40
(C)  70
(D) 110

**GO ON TO THE NEXT PAGE**

**10.** Ali buys 10 burgers and 7 chocolate milkshakes for $50.95. If the price of a chocolate milkshake is $0.25 cheaper than the price of a burger, what is the price of a chocolate milkshake?

(A) $2.85
(B) $3.10
(C) $4.05
(D) $5.09

**11.** The acute angles of a right triangle have a ratio of 12 to 3. What is the difference between the two angle measures?

(A) 42 degrees
(B) 54 degrees
(C) 64 degrees
(D) 72 degrees

**12.** A number is a palindrome if it can be written the same backwards and forwards (6336 is an example of a palindrome). What number divides into every 4 digit palindrome?

(A)  2
(B)  3
(C)  7
(D) 11

| Day | Number of books |
|---|---|
| Monday | $x$ |
| Tuesday | $2x$ |
| Wednesday | $0.5x$ |
| Thursday | $x$ |
| Friday | $3.5x$ |

**13.** The above table outlines how many books Anthony reads per day in terms of $x$. What was the average daily number of books that Anthony reads, in terms of $x$?

(A) $\dfrac{5x}{8}$

(B) $x$

(C) $\dfrac{8x}{5}$

(D) $8x$

$$x^2 - 1 < x^3$$

**14.** For which of the following values is the above inequality true?

(A) $x = -3$
(B) $x = -2$
(C) $x = -1$
(D) $x = 0$

**GO ON TO THE NEXT PAGE**

Growth of Bacteria Populations

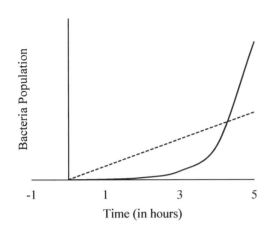

Time (in hours)

**15.** Bacteria $A$ is represented by the solid line and Bacteria $B$ is represented by the dotted line in the graph shown above. Which of the following statements is TRUE?

(A) Bacteria $A$ is growing at a linear rate
(B) Bacteria $B$ is growing at an exponential rate
(C) Neither Bacteria $A$ nor Bacteria $B$ is growing at a linear rate
(D) Bacteria $B$ is growing linearly, but Bacteria $A$ is growing exponentially

**16.** Which of the following values of $x$ results in the largest value of $y$ in the equation $y = -(x - 2)^2 + 4$?

(A) –2
(B) 0
(C) 2
(D) 4

$$x = 12$$
$$3x = 4y^2$$

**17.** In the system of equations above, if $y > 0$, what is the value of $x^2y$?

(A) 36
(B) 108
(C) 432
(D) 1296

**18.** The product of two positive consecutive even numbers is 168. What is the smaller of the two numbers?

(A) 24
(B) 21
(C) 14
(D) 12

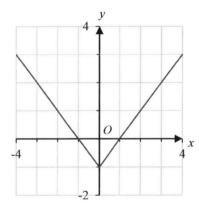

**19.** The function $f(x)$ is graphed above. If $g(x) = f(x) - 1$, which of the following statements is TRUE?

(A) $g(x)$ is greater than or equal to zero.
(B) $g(x)$ is greater than or equal to negative one.
(C) $g(x)$ is greater than or equal to negative two.
(D) $g(x)$ is greater than negative one, but smaller than five.

**GO ON TO THE NEXT PAGE**

**20.** Three different integers are randomly selected from a group of five unique integers consisting of 1 through 5. What is the probability that these numbers are 1, 2, and 3?

(A) One in five
(B) One in ten
(C) One in twenty
(D) One in sixty

**21.** The ratio of $d{:}c$ is 3:1. If the sum of $d$ and $c$ is $s$, what is the value for $d$, in terms of $s$?

(A) $\dfrac{4}{3}s$

(B) $\dfrac{3}{4}s$

(C) $s-3$

(D) $s-4$

**Questions 22 and 23 refer to the following information.**

A survey on coffee consumption was conducted among a random sample of students at a university. A total of 200 students were surveyed. The table below displays a summary of the results.

| Cups of Coffee (Per Day) | | | | |
|---|---|---|---|---|
| Student Year | 0 | 1 | 2 or more | Total |
| Freshman | 25 | 9 | 16 | 50 |
| Sophomore | 5 | 19 | 26 | 50 |
| Junior | 10 | 6 | 50 | 66 |
| Senior | 0 | 2 | 32 | 34 |
| Total | 40 | 36 | 124 | 200 |

**22.** Based on the information in the table, who would be least likely to drink any cups of coffee during the day?

(A) a freshman
(B) a sophomore
(C) a junior
(D) a senior

**23.** Which of the following statements about the students surveyed is not supported by the table above?

(A) A higher percentage of juniors than sophomores drink 2 or more cups of coffee per day.
(B) A higher percentage of juniors than seniors drink 2 or more cups of coffee per day.
(C) 20% of all students surveyed do not drink coffee.
(D) 50% of the freshmen do not drink coffee.

GO ON TO THE NEXT PAGE

Number of Passengers Using the Commuter Line

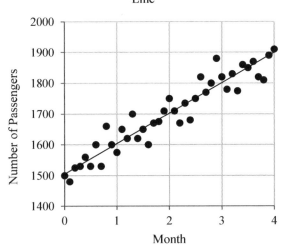

| Produce at the Farmer's Market | |
|---|---|
| Fruit | Price |
| Apples | 3 for 2 dollars |
| Peaches | 1 for 1 dollar |
| Oranges | 4 for 3 dollars |

**24.** The graph above shows the number of passengers on a train line over 4 months. If $m$ is the number of months, which of the following functions best represents the graph's line of best fit?

(A) $f(m) = 200 + 1500m$
(B) $f(m) = 150 + 100m$
(C) $f(m) = 1500 + 100m$
(D) $f(m) = 150m + 1500$

**25.** The chart above shows the prices for fruit at a farmer's market. Claire spends 4 dollars on apples, 2 dollars on peaches, and 3 dollars on oranges and puts all of her fruits in a brown bag. If she randomly selects a fruit from her bag, what is the probability she grabs an apple?

(A) $\dfrac{1}{4}$

(B) $\dfrac{1}{3}$

(C) $\dfrac{1}{2}$

(D) $\dfrac{2}{3}$

**26.** $j$ is equal to 925 and $k$ is equal to 5,550. A number, $n$, is added to $j$, such that the ratio of $j + n$ to $k$ is 1:3. What is the ratio of $n$ to $j + n$, expressed as a percentage of $j + n$?

(A) 30%
(B) 40%
(C) 50%
(D) 60%

GO ON TO THE NEXT PAGE

**27.** When Amelia goes cliff diving in Bali, her height above the water can be modelled by the function $f(t) = -2t^2 + 4t + 30$ , where $t$ represents time in seconds. How long, in seconds, does it take for Amelia to hit the water?

(A) 3
(B) 4
(C) 5
(D) 6

Number of Foreign Languages Offered in a High School Curriculum

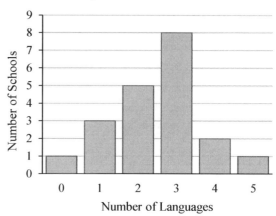

**28.** The average of 5 positive numbers is 85. If the highest of these numbers is 100, which of the following statements CANNOT be true?

(A) The lowest score is 20.
(B) The highest range possible is 75.
(C) The median is greater than 25.
(D) The mode is 85.

**29.** 20 high schools were surveyed on the number of languages offered in their curriculum. The results are shown in the chart above. How many schools offer fewer languages than average across the 20 schools?

(A)  9
(B)  10
(C)  11
(D)  17

**30.** A city wants to replace 10% of its bus fleet with hydrogen-powered buses. Each hydrogen-powered bus costs $200,000. If there are 180 buses in the city, how much money, in dollars, will it cost for the city to meet its goal?

(A) 1,800,000
(B) 2,000,000
(C) 3,600,000
(D) 4,000,000

GO ON TO THE NEXT PAGE

Practice Test 1

Unapproved reproduction or distribution
of any portion of this material is unlawful.

**Directions:** For questions 31-37, fill out your answers using the grids in Section 4 of your answer sheet.

You will need to enter your answers for the following questions in the grids provided in your answer sheet.

- Make sure to fill in bubbles completely.
- Mark no more than one circle in any column.
- Answers written in the boxes above the grid are *not* scored.
- You can write your answer into those boxes as a guide when you bubble in your answers, however, remember that you always need to bubble your answers as well!

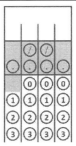

**Placement:**

You can start your answer in any column as long as you can fit in the whole answer.

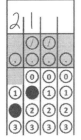 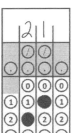 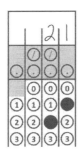

**Reminders:**

- Some grid-in problems have more than one correct answer. In those cases, you may grid in any of the possible answers as long as it fits in the grid.
- If you get a decimal answer with more digits than can fit in the grid, round your answer but make sure that it fills the entire grid.

**Mixed Numbers:**

There is no negative sign in the grid, so all answers will be positive numbers or zero. You can grid proper and improper fractions, but *not* mixed numbers. For example, the mixed number $3\frac{1}{4}$ must be written as 13/4 or 3.25. If you grid the answer as the mixed number 31/4, the machine will read it as $\frac{31}{4}$, which is incorrect.

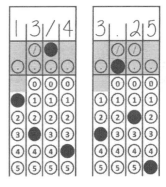

**GO ON TO THE NEXT PAGE**

**31.** If $2x$ is equal to the sum of 11, 12, and 13, what is the value of $x$?

$$-15(2 + n) = -16(n - 7)$$

**32.** What is the value of $n$ in the equation above?

**33.** If $x$ is 60% of $y$, and $y$ is 30% of $z$, $x$ is what percent of $z$?

$$8^{3x-1} = \frac{1}{4^{3x-21}}$$

**34.** What is the value of $x$ in the equation above?

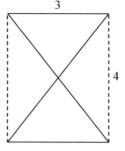

**35.** A rectangle has side lengths 3 and 4 as shown in the figure above. What is the total length of the solid lines?

**GO ON TO THE NEXT PAGE**

**36.** What is the radius of the circle with the equation $x^2 + y^2 - 7 = 9$?

**Questions 37 and 38 refer to the following information.**

Susan is training for a marathon. To track her progress, she has been keeping a record of her recent practice runs. The table below summarizes her training progress.

| Time For Practice Runs | | |
|---|---|---|
| Week | Distance (in miles) | Time (in minutes) |
| 1 | 10 | 100 |
| 2 | 12 | 108 |
| 3 | 8 | 68 |
| 4 | 10 | 87 |
| 5 | 12 | 105 |

**37.** How much faster, in seconds, did Susan run each mile in Week 3 compared to Week 4?

**38.** Susan would like to run 26 miles in 3 hours and 54 minutes. Currently, she can run 26 miles at a pace of 11 minutes/mile. If she plans on improving her pace by 15 seconds/mile every week, how many weeks will it take Susan to reach her goal?

# STOP

**If you complete the problem set before time elapses, you may review your responses for this section.**

**Do not view or begin working on any other sections.**

# Section 5

Unapproved reproduction or distribution of any portion of this material is unlawful.

# SECTION 5

## Time – 50 minutes

---

**Turn to Section 5 of your answer sheet to write your essay.**

---

**Important Reminders:**

- You have 50 minutes to write your essay.
- A pencil is required for the essay. An essay written in ink will receive a score of zero.
- Do not write your essay in your test book. You will receive credit only for what you write on your answer sheet.
- Write legibly.

**As you read the passage below, consider how Frank Pasquale uses**

- evidence, such as facts or examples, to support claims.
- reasoning to develop ideas and to connect claims and evidence.
- stylistic or persuasive elements, such as word choice or appeals to emotion, to add power to the ideas expressed.

---

*Adapted from Frank Pasquale, "The Dark Market for Personal Data," © 2014 by The New York Times Company. Originally published October 16, 2014.*

The reputation business is exploding. Having eroded privacy for decades, shady, poorly regulated data miners, brokers and resellers have now taken creepy classification to a whole new level....

There are lists of "impulse buyers." Lists of suckers: gullible consumers who have shown that they are susceptible to "vulnerability-based marketing." And lists of those deemed commercially undesirable because they live in or near trailer parks or nursing homes. Not to mention lists of people who have been accused of wrongdoing, even if they were not charged or convicted.

Typically sold at a few cents per name, the lists don't have to be particularly reliable to attract eager buyers — mostly marketers, but also, increasingly, financial institutions vetting customers to guard against fraud, and employers screening potential hires.

There are three problems with these lists. First, they are often inaccurate. For example, as The Washington Post reported, an Arkansas woman found her credit history and job prospects wrecked after she was mistakenly listed as a

methamphetamine dealer. It took her years to clear her name and find a job.

Second, even when the information is accurate, many of the lists have no business being in the hands of retailers, bosses or banks. Having a medical condition, or having been a victim of a crime, is simply not relevant to most employment or credit decisions.

Third, people aren't told they are on these lists, so they have no opportunity to correct bad information. The Arkansas woman found out about the inaccurate report only when she was denied a job. She was one of the rare ones.

"Data-driven" hiring practices are under increasing scrutiny, because the data may be a proxy for race, class or disability. For example, in 2011, CVS settled a charge of disability discrimination after a job applicant challenged a personality test that probed mental health issues. But if an employer were to secretly use lists based on inferences about mental health, it would be nearly impossible for an affected applicant to find out what was going on. Secrecy is discrimination's best friend: Unknown unfairness can never be detected, let alone corrected.

These problems can't be solved with existing law. The Federal Trade Commission has strained to understand

**GO ON TO THE NEXT PAGE**

personal data markets — a $156-billion-a-year industry — and it can't find out where the data brokers get their information, and whom they sell it to. Hiding behind a veil of trade secrecy, most refuse to divulge this vital information....

It's unrealistic to expect individuals to inquire, broker by broker, about their files. Instead, we need to require brokers to make targeted disclosures to consumers. Uncovering problems in Big Data (or decision models based on that data) should not be a burden we expect individuals to solve on their own.

Privacy protections in other areas of the law can and should be extended to cover consumer data. The Health Insurance Portability and Accountability Act, or Hipaa, obliges doctors and hospitals to give patients access to their records. The Fair Credit Reporting Act gives loan and job applicants, among others, a right to access, correct and annotate files maintained by credit reporting agencies.

It is time to modernize these laws by applying them to all companies that peddle sensitive personal information. If the laws cover only a narrow range of entities, they may as well be dead letters. For example, protections in Hipaa don't govern the "health profiles" that are compiled and traded by data brokers, which can learn a great deal about our health even without access to medical records.

Congress should require data brokers to register with the Federal Trade Commission, and allow individuals to request immediate notification once they have been placed on lists that contain sensitive data. Reputable data brokers will want to respond to good-faith complaints, to make their lists more accurate. Plaintiffs' lawyers could use defamation law to hold recalcitrant firms accountable.

We need regulation to help consumers recognize the perils of the new information landscape without being overwhelmed with data. The right to be notified about the use of one's data and the right to challenge and correct errors is fundamental. Without these protections, we'll continue to be judged by a big-data Star Chamber of unaccountable decision makers using questionable sources.

---

**Assignment:** Write an essay in which you explain how Frank Pasquale builds an argument to persuade his audience that privacy laws should be updated to regulate the modern data industry. In your essay, analyze how Pasquale uses one or more of the features listed in the box above (or features of your own choice) to strengthen the logic and persuasiveness of his argument. Be sure that your analysis focuses on the most relevant features of the passage.

Your essay should not explain whether you agree with Pasquale's claims, but rather explain how Pasquale builds an argument to persuade his audience.

# Part 3
# **Answers and Scoring**

# ANSWERS

## SECTION 1: READING

| | | | |
|---|---|---|---|
| 1. C | 14. D | 27. A | 40. C |
| 2. B | 15. B | 28. C | 41. A |
| 3. A | 16. A | 29. B | 42. B |
| 4. A | 17. A | 30. B | 43. B |
| 5. D | 18. C | 31. C | 44. B |
| 6. B | 19. B | 32. D | 45. A |
| 7. C | 20. D | 33. D | 46. C |
| 8. D | 21. D | 34. D | 47. A |
| 9. C | 22. B | 35. A | 48. B |
| 10. D | 23. B | 36. B | 49. C |
| 11. A | 24. B | 37. A | 50. D |
| 12. B | 25. C | 38. B | 51. D |
| 13. B | 26. A | 39. C | 52. C |

## SECTION 2: MATH (NO-CALCULATOR)

| | | | |
|---|---|---|---|
| 1. C | 6. B | 11. B | 16. 3 |
| 2. C | 7. A | 12. B | 17. 10 |
| 3. B | 8. B | 13. D | 18. 17/2 |
| 4. C | 9. C | 14. A | 19. 6 |
| 5. D | 10. A | 15. B | 20. 6 |

## Section 3: Writing

| | | | |
|---|---|---|---|
| 1. A | 12. C | 23. B | 34. B |
| 2. C | 13. C | 24. C | 35. A |
| 3. B | 14. B | 25. C | 36. C |
| 4. C | 15. C | 26. B | 37. D |
| 5. D | 16. A | 27. D | 38. C |
| 6. B | 17. D | 28. A | 39. A |
| 7. B | 18. C | 29. D | 40. D |
| 8. B | 19. C | 30. B | 41. D |
| 9. C | 20. D | 31. A | 42. C |
| 10. C | 21. D | 32. B | 43. B |
| 11. D | 22. A | 33. B | 44. B |

## Section 4: Math (calculator)

| | | | |
|---|---|---|---|
| 1. B | 11. B | 21. B | 31. 18 |
| 2. B | 12. D | 22. A | 32. 142 |
| 3. B | 13. C | 23. B | 33. 18 |
| 4. B | 14. D | 24. C | 34. 3 |
| 5. D | 15. D | 25. C | 35. 16 |
| 6. B | 16. C | 26. C | 36. 4 |
| 7. D | 17. C | 27. C | 37. 12 |
| 8. B | 18. D | 28. A | 38. 8 |
| 9. C | 19. C | 29. A | |
| 10. A | 20. B | 30. C | |

Download printable answer sheets, answer keys, and Excel scoring sheets from:

ivyglobal.com/study

# THE SCORING SYSTEM
## SECTION 2

The new SAT will have three **test scores** on a scale from 10 to 40. There will be one test score for each test: the Reading Test, the Writing Test, and the Math Test. The Reading Test score and the Writing and Language Test score will be added together and converted to a single **area score** in Evidence-Based Reading and Writing; there will also be an area score in Math based on the Math Test Score.

The area scores will be on a scale from 200 to 800. Added together, they will form the **composite score** for the whole test, on a scale from 400 to 1600. The Essay will be scored separately and will not affect your scores in other areas.

| SAT Scoring | |
|---|---|
| Test Scores (10 to 40) | • Reading Test<br>• Writing Test<br>• Math Test |
| Area Scores (200 to 800) | • Evidence-Based Reading and Writing<br>• Math |
| Composite Score (400 to 1600) | • Math (Area Score) + Evidence-Based Reading and Writing (Area Score) |
| Essay Scores (1 to 4) | • Reading<br>• Analysis<br>• Writing |

The College Board will also be reporting new types of scores. **Cross-test scores** for **Analysis in Science** and **Analysis in History/Social Studies** will be based on performance on specific questions across different tests relating to specific types of content. For example, your cross-test score in Analysis in Science will be based on your performance on questions relating to science passages on the Reading Test as well as questions using scientific data on the Math Test. These scores will be on a scale from 10 to 40.

There will also be seven **subscores** based on particular question types within each test section. Subscores will be reported on a scale from 1 to 15. Four will be related to particular questions in the Reading and Writing Test: Words in Context, Command of Evidence, Expression of Ideas, and Standard English Conventions. The other three relate to specific types of questions on the Math Test: Heart of Algebra, Problem Solving and Data Analysis, and Passport to Advanced Math.

# CROSS-TEST SCORES AND SUBSCORES

You will receive **cross-test scores** for Analysis in Science and Analysis in History/Social Studies. The scores are based on your performance on questions in their respective subject domains across all sections of the exam. These scores will be reported on a scale of 10-40.

You will also receive **subscores** based on your performance on certain question types within each test section. Subscores will be reported on a scale of 1-15. There will be seven subscores, for the following areas:

- **Words in Context:** this subscore will be based on your performance on questions related to determining the meanings of words in the context of a passage in the English area.

- **Command of Evidence:** this subscore will be based on your performance on questions that ask you to identify the best evidence in the Reading and Writing tests.

- **Expression of Ideas:** this subscore will be based on your performance on questions that ask you to identify clear, stylistically appropriate choices in writing passages.

- **Standard English Conventions:** this subscore will be based on your performance on questions that ask you to identify and correct errors of grammar, punctuation, usage, and syntax in writing passages.

- **Heart of Algebra:** this subscore will be based on your performance on Math questions testing key concepts in Algebra.

- **Problem Solving and Data Analysis**: this subscore will be based on your performance on Math questions testing your ability to analyze sets of data, the meanings of units and quantities, and the properties of different objects and operations.

- **Passport to Advanced Math:** this subscore will be based on your performance on Math questions that test the skills you'll build on as you continue to learn more advanced math including rewriting expressions, solving quadratic equations, working with polynomials and radicals, and solving systems of equations.

As of our publication date, the College Board had not released detailed information on how these scores will be calculated.

# SCORING YOUR TEST
## SECTION 3

To score your tests, first use the answer key to mark each of your responses right or wrong. Then, calculate your **raw score** for each section by counting up the number of correct responses. Use the tables below to help you calculate your scores:

**Raw Score**

| Section | # of Questions Correct |
|---|---|
| 1. Reading | _____ |
| 2. Math: No-Calculator | _____ |
| 3. Writing | _____ |
| 4. Math: Calculator | _____ |

**Raw Score for Reading (Section 1):** _____

**Raw Score for Writing (Section 3):** _____

**Raw Score for Math (Section 2 + 4):** _____

## SCALED SCORES

Once you have found your raw score for each section, convert it into an approximate **scaled test score** using the following charts. To find a scaled test score for each section, find the row in the Raw Score column which corresponds to your raw score for that section, then check the column for the section you are scoring in the same row. For example, if you had a raw score of 48 for reading, then your scaled reading test score would be 39. Keep in mind that these scaled scores are estimates only. Your actual SAT score will be scaled against the scores of all other high school students taking the test on your test date.

| Raw Score | Math Scaled Score | Reading Scaled Score | Writing Scaled Score | Raw Score | Math Scaled Score | Reading Scaled Score | Writing Scaled Score |
|---|---|---|---|---|---|---|---|
| 58 | 40 | | | 28 | 23 | 26 | 25 |
| 57 | 40 | | | 27 | 22 | 25 | 24 |
| 56 | 40 | | | 26 | 22 | 25 | 24 |
| 55 | 39 | | | 25 | 21 | 24 | 23 |
| 54 | 38 | | | 24 | 21 | 24 | 23 |
| 53 | 37 | | | 23 | 20 | 23 | 22 |
| 52 | 36 | 40 | | 22 | 20 | 22 | 21 |
| 51 | 35 | 40 | | 21 | 19 | 22 | 21 |
| 50 | 34 | 40 | | 20 | 19 | 21 | 20 |
| 49 | 34 | 39 | | 19 | 18 | 20 | 20 |
| 48 | 33 | 39 | | 18 | 18 | 20 | 19 |
| 47 | 33 | 38 | | 17 | 17 | 19 | 19 |
| 46 | 32 | 37 | | 16 | 16 | 19 | 18 |
| 45 | 32 | 36 | | 15 | 15 | 18 | 18 |
| 44 | 31 | 35 | 40 | 14 | 14 | 17 | 17 |
| 43 | 30 | 34 | 39 | 13 | 13 | 16 | 16 |
| 42 | 30 | 34 | 38 | 12 | 12 | 16 | 15 |
| 41 | 29 | 33 | 37 | 11 | 11 | 14 | 14 |
| 40 | 29 | 33 | 35 | 10 | 10 | 13 | 13 |
| 39 | 28 | 32 | 34 | 9 | 10 | 12 | 12 |
| 38 | 28 | 31 | 33 | 8 | 10 | 11 | 11 |
| 37 | 27 | 31 | 32 | 7 | 10 | 10 | 10 |
| 36 | 27 | 30 | 31 | 6 | 10 | 10 | 10 |
| 35 | 26 | 30 | 30 | 5 | 10 | 10 | 10 |
| 34 | 26 | 29 | 29 | 4 | 10 | 10 | 10 |
| 33 | 25 | 29 | 28 | 3 | 10 | 10 | 10 |
| 32 | 25 | 28 | 27 | 2 | 10 | 10 | 10 |
| 31 | 24 | 28 | 27 | 1 | 10 | 10 | 10 |
| 30 | 24 | 27 | 26 | 0 | 10 | 10 | 10 |
| 29 | 23 | 26 | 26 | | | | |

Use the table below to record your scaled scores:

| Scaled Scores | |
|---|---|
| Scaled Score for Reading (Out of 40): | _____ |
| Scaled Score for Writing (Out of 40): | _____ |
| Scaled Score for Math (Out of 40): | _____ |

## ESSAY SCORE

Review the essay scoring criteria in Chapter 4. Then, estimate your essay score by assigning your essay a score out of 1-4 in each scoring area, using the following charts as a guide. Have a trusted reader check your work.

| | Essay Score | |
|---|---|---|
| Scoring Area | Reader 1 Score (1-4) | Reader 2 Score (1-4) |
| Reading | _____ | _____ |
| Analysis | _____ | _____ |
| Writing | _____ | _____ |

# AREA SCORE CONVERSION

You can look up your area score out of 800 below. To find your overall score, combine your area score for Reading + Writing with your area score for Math to get your total score out of 1600.

## READING + WRITING

| Scaled Score | Area Score | Scaled Score | Area Score | Scaled Score | Area Score |
|:---:|:---:|:---:|:---:|:---:|:---:|
| 80 | 760-800 | 59 | 550-630 | 39 | 350-430 |
| 79 | 750-800 | 58 | 540-620 | 38 | 340-420 |
| 78 | 740-800 | 57 | 530-610 | 37 | 330-410 |
| 77 | 730-800 | 56 | 520-600 | 36 | 320-400 |
| 76 | 720-800 | 55 | 510-590 | 35 | 310-390 |
| 75 | 710-790 | 54 | 500-580 | 34 | 300-380 |
| 74 | 700-780 | 53 | 490-570 | 33 | 290-370 |
| 73 | 690-770 | 52 | 480-560 | 32 | 280-360 |
| 72 | 680-760 | 51 | 470-550 | 31 | 270-350 |
| 71 | 670-750 | 50 | 460-540 | 30 | 260-340 |
| 70 | 660-740 | 49 | 450-530 | 29 | 250-330 |
| 69 | 650-730 | 48 | 440-520 | 28 | 240-320 |
| 68 | 640-720 | 47 | 430-510 | 27 | 230-310 |
| 67 | 630-710 | 46 | 420-500 | 26 | 220-300 |
| 66 | 620-700 | 45 | 410-490 | 25 | 210-290 |
| 65 | 610-690 | 44 | 400-480 | 24 | 200-280 |
| 64 | 600-680 | 43 | 390-470 | 23 | 200-270 |
| 63 | 590-670 | 42 | 380-460 | 22 | 200-260 |
| 62 | 580-660 | 41 | 370-450 | 21 | 200-250 |
| 61 | 570-650 | 40 | 360-440 | 20 | 200-240 |
| 60 | 560-640 |  |  |  |  |

## MATH

| Total Points | Area Score | Total Points | Area Score |
|:---:|:---:|:---:|:---:|
| 40 | 760-800 | 24 | 440-520 |
| 39 | 740-800 | 23 | 420-500 |
| 38 | 720-800 | 22 | 400-480 |
| 37 | 700-780 | 21 | 380-460 |
| 36 | 680-760 | 20 | 360-440 |
| 35 | 660-740 | 19 | 340-420 |
| 34 | 640-720 | 18 | 320-400 |
| 33 | 620-700 | 17 | 300-380 |
| 32 | 600-680 | 16 | 280-360 |
| 31 | 580-660 | 15 | 260-340 |
| 30 | 560-640 | 14 | 240-320 |
| 29 | 540-620 | 13 | 220-300 |
| 28 | 520-600 | 12 | 200-280 |
| 27 | 500-580 | 11 | 200-260 |
| 26 | 480-560 | 10 | 200-240 |
| 25 | 460-540 | | |

Use the table below to record your area scores and to calculate your overall score:

| Reading + Writing Area Score | | Math Area Score | | Overall Score (400-1600) |
|:---:|:---:|:---:|:---:|:---:|
| _____ | + | _____ | = | _____ |

21667041R00049

Made in the USA
San Bernardino, CA
31 May 2015